PICTORIAL HISTORY
HAWKESBURY

MICHELLE NICHOLS

KINGSCLEAR BOOKS

FRONT COVER PHOTOGRAPH:
Looking across Windsor Bridge to the township of
Windsor in 1879.
(GPO ML SLNSW)

BACK COVER PHOTOGRAPH:
A Hawkesbury picnic in the 1890s with very posed subjects
sitting still for the photographer.
(WC ML SLNSW)

In loving memory of Ernest Nichols 1932 — 2004

Kingsclear Books ABN 99 001 904 034
kingsclearbooks@gmail.com
www.kingsclearbooks.com.au
P.O. Box 335 Alexandria 1435

Phone (02) 9557 4367

First printed 2004, revised and reprinted 2005, 2016, 2021
Printed in China by Red Planet Print Management

LIST OF ABBREVIATIONS

BC	Bilpin Collection
GPO	Government Printing Office
HCCLS	Hawkesbury City Council Library Service
ML	Mitchell Library
NLA	National Library of Australia
RAAF	Royal Australian Air Force
SLNSW	State Library of NSW
SRA	State Rail Authority
SRNSW	State Records of NSW
UWS	University of Western Sydney – Hawkesbury
WC	Woodhill Collection

ACKNOWLEDGEMENTS

The Hawkesbury district is filled with wonderful memories of the past. There are reminders all over the landscape: a sandstone building, a cemetery of many pioneers, a crumbling ruin. Sometimes it is easy to close your eyes and imagine the busy scene at Thompson Square, the farmers ploughing the fields on the lowlands, a boat sail on the Hawkesbury or the wing of a primitive plane flying over Ham Common.

I feel it is important to acknowledge the recorders of local history in the Hawkesbury district. To those who put their memories onto paper and to those in the more recent past, who have researched and produced quality publications. Also without the photographers of the past, history would be uninspiring. With photographs it is easier for us to see the past.

Firstly, I would like to thank Catherine Warne for her tremendous series of pictorial histories that are a significant contribution to Australian history. With very special thanks to all of my family (especially my four sisters) and also to my new family, for their love and support. Special thanks to my parents, Ern and Joyce who in my childhood encouraged my enthusiasm for history. With thanks to my friends at Hawkesbury City Council Library where I work. Particular mention of Robynne Winley and Cathy McHardy for their special efforts. To my soul mate, Jonathan Auld, whom I found unexpectedly, thank you for sharing your life so completely, and my passion for history, also for your assistance with this production.

I would also like to acknowledge the wonderful photographic collection of Hawkesbury City Council Library Service and the collections of D. G. Bowd, Barney Morley and R. D. Power. Also for information and/or photographs my thanks to: Jonathan Auld, Ted Books, Lorna Campbell, Carol Carruthers, Marj Clarke, Graham Clayton, Coral Cleary, Judith and June Clemson, Arthur Cooper, Bev Douglass, Owen and Jan Earle, Graham and Carol Edds, Meredyth Hungerford, Chris McLachlan, Louise McMahon, National Museum of Australia, Rosemary Phillis, Verna Powe, Fay and John Priora, Jean Purtell, Royal Australian Air Force, State Library of NSW, State Records NSW, Alan Strachan and family, UWS Hawkesbury, Tizzana Winery and Fay Worrell.

If you have any photographs of the Hawkesbury and would like to share the images, the council has facilities for copying. Contact Hawkesbury City Council Library, Email library@hawkesbury.nsw.gov.au for more details or write c/– PO Box 146, Windsor 2756 NSW

A horticultural development on the Hawkesbury in 1928. (GPO ML SLNSW)

FOREWORD

The Hawkesbury district in Sydney's west was once home to many Australians and in the early 19th century had the second highest population in the colony. For the first few decades of the 1800s it was one of the major settlements alongside Sydney and Parramatta. During the 19th and early 20th century many fine buildings were established throughout the Hawkesbury district and fortunately a significant number have survived. There are almost 700 items registered on the State Heritage Inventory from the Hawkesbury with about 10 per cent of these considered important enough to be listed: Ebenezer, Greenway's masterpiece St Matthew's Anglican Church, Windsor, and the oldest building used as a hotel in Australia, the Macquarie Arms in Windsor. For over two centuries it has been the home to numerous people and many have travelled the rivers and roads within the Hawkesbury district. Indeed many Australians can trace their origins (both convict and free) to this district. The Hawkesbury was, and still is, a fashionable tourist destination however there are many places within the district that are generally not explored.

Before the middle of the century had passed, the colony had become self sufficient and as free settlers were encouraged, the population grew and the settlement spread. The importance of the Hawkesbury district had waned but for its settlers it took on an air of permanence. With new flood-free pastures available in the west and the lure of the gold rushes, the course of the Hawkesbury district changed. Agriculture and commercial ventures continued to develop, albeit slowly, throughout the district. The townships of Windsor and Richmond were the main administrative centres with the necessary amenities and recreational facilities. With the exception of the expansion of the rail service, and the focus moving away from the river, the pace of life changed little in the Hawkesbury. The continual impact of floods also put a dampener on things.

With Federation in 1901, a new era of government began. By the turn of the century children had the opportunity to be educated with most localities in the Hawkesbury having access to schools. Technology was making life that much easier. Access to motor cars and aeroplanes resulted with persons travelling further afield. Small industries prospered. Wars had a big impact on the Hawkesbury community in the 20th century, the Boer War, as well as World War I and II. Post World War II many migrants made the Hawkesbury district their home.

There are a number of problems facing the Hawkesbury today. Issues such as water quality is still a vital concern, as well as the urban sprawl reaching the Hawkesbury region. Residents are concerned with the balance between the environment and the needs of the community. Social issues such as health and crime are high on the agenda. Lack of public transport in the Hawkesbury is a hindrance to the community. Conserving our heritage still matters to the people of the Hawkesbury. It gives a sense of community, connection and belonging to the place where we live.

Michelle Nichols

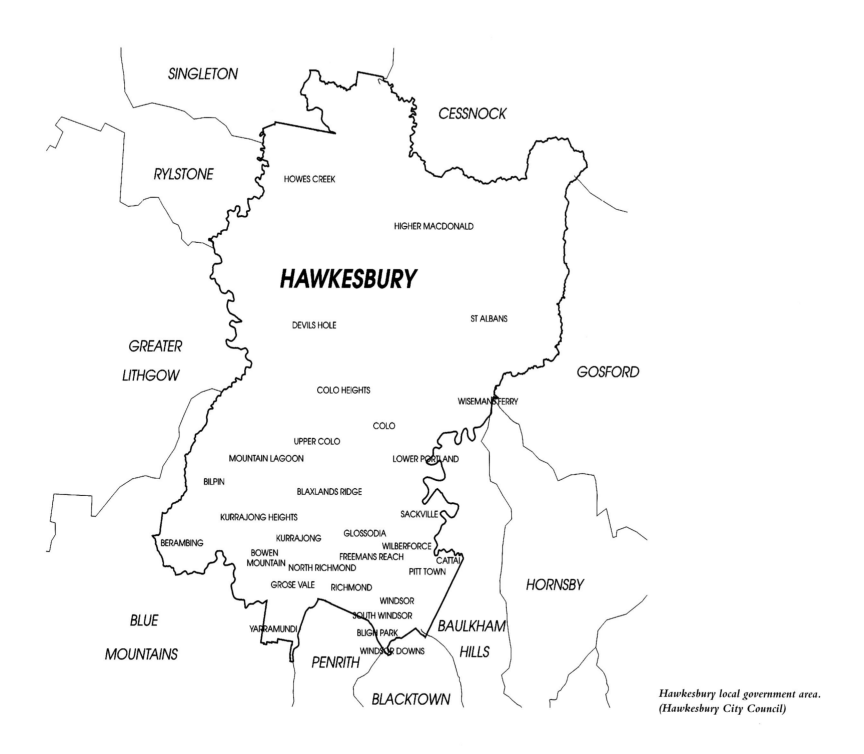

SINGLETON

CESSNOCK

RYLSTONE

HOWES CREEK

HIGHER MACDONALD

HAWKESBURY

GREATER

LITHGOW

DEVILS HOLE

ST ALBANS

GOSFORD

COLO HEIGHTS

WISEMANS FERRY

COLO

UPPER COLO

LOWER PORTLAND

MOUNTAIN LAGOON

BILPIN

BLAXLANDS RIDGE

KURRAJONG HEIGHTS

SACKVILLE

GLOSSODIA

BERAMBING

KURRAJONG

WILBERFORCE

BOWEN
MOUNTAIN

FREEMANS REACH

CATTAI

NORTH RICHMOND

PITT TOWN

GROSE VALE

RICHMOND

HORNSBY

WINDSOR

BLUE

SOUTH WINDSOR

YARRAMUNDI

BLIGH PARK

BAULKHAM

MOUNTAINS

WINDSOR DOWNS

HILLS

PENRITH

BLACKTOWN

Hawkesbury local government area.
(Hawkesbury City Council)

LIST OF CONTENTS

SETTING THE SCENE

Hawkesbury City Council covers a vast area, from Vineyard to St Albans, and Bilpin to Londonderry. It is the largest Local Government Area in the Sydney region, with a total of 2793 square kilometres. The Hawkesbury district includes the incredible river system, national parks, some with World Heritage wilderness areas, and unique bushland. The river confusingly begins at the Nepean River, winds its way out past Castlereagh, on to Windsor and Richmond, past Wisemans Ferry and on to the mouth at Broken Bay near Brooklyn. Other notable waterways, such as the Grose, Colo and Macdonald rivers feed into the Hawkesbury and a number of major creek systems enter at various points such as Cattai, Wheeny, Webbs, Mangrove, Berowra and South creeks. Topography varies from floodplains and forests to urban and commercial zones. The native vegetation is diverse.

The Hawkesbury district is home to 62 353 people, with <1 percent annual growth rate, according to the 2011 Census. Most people live around the urban centres of Windsor, together with South Windsor and Bligh Park, plus Richmond and North Richmond.

ABOVE:
Clearing the land at Ham Common in the 1890s. (UWS)

OPPOSITE:
Hawkesbury Valley seen in flood in 1990. (RAAF)

LEFT:
A cottage and barn on South Creek, near the bridge on Windsor Road in 1979, have since disappeared. (HCCLS)

ORIGINAL OCCUPANTS

For at least 30 000 years, Aborigines have occupied parts of Western Sydney. The Darug and Darkinung tribes of Aborigines were the original occupants. The Darug tribe, also known as Dharug or Daruk, was made up of smaller groups of Aborigines who wandered over the area known as the Cumberland Plains, covering the territory from the mouth of the Hawkesbury River, westwards to Mount Victoria, east to Sydney and south to Camden and Liverpool.

Another tribe, known as the Darkinung, lived in the area bounded by Wilberforce and Wisemans Ferry on the Hawkesbury River through to Singleton and the Hunter Valley and travelled south to the Macdonald and Colo Rivers area. Aborigines from the Sydney area to the Blue Mountains and Hawkesbury spoke different dialects unique to various areas. Fortunately remnants of these languages have survived.

The river called Derrubbin (or Venrubben) was critical to the indigenous tribes as a source of food and transport route. South Creek, originally known as Wianamatta, was also essential to the local tribes. Fish, eels mussels, water birds and wild yams were the main food source. Bark canoes were used for transport. On the sandstone platforms Aborigines engraved animals, mythological figures and simple motifs or drew with ochre and charcoal. Stone made axes, barbs, grinders, points and scrapers. Within each tribe were smaller groups, known as a 'band' or 'clan' of Aborigines. Groups were named after localities such as Boorooberongal (Richmond clan), Caddie (Cattai-Pitt Town clan), Gomerigal (South Creek clan) and the Kurrajong tribe. With the arrival of the First Fleet in 1788 diseases decimated the indigenous population.

In 1789 the first exploration party of the Hawkesbury River led by Governor Phillip noted signs of the Aborigines everywhere, including their canoes 'which consists of nothing more than a large piece of bark, bent in the middle, and open at both ends' as well as traps and bird decoys. In 1791 a larger party including Governor Phillip, Captains John Hunter and Watkin Tench, as well as two Sydney Aborigines, Colebee and Balladerry, tried to establish whether the Hawkesbury and Nepean were the same river. They met up with a small group of local Aborigines from the Boorooberongal clan which the Sydney guides described as 'climbers of trees'. The older man provided a demonstration by cutting notches into a tree (used as toe grips) and then nimbly climbing. Gifts were exchanged and three of them joined the party, Gombeeree, his son Yellomundee (or Yarramundi) and grandson Djimba. The remainder of the families stayed at a distance. Tench was most impressed with their calm, trusting nature towards the Europeans.

From the beginning there was conflict between the two groups. When farms were granted the local tribes found their access to the river and their food supply was blocked. They retaliated by ransacking property, burning crops and killing

Aboriginal hand stencils in the Hawkesbury district. (BC HCCLS)

animals. There were also recordings of deaths and murders on both sides. The NSW Corps was sent to investigate. Contemporary accounts state that some of the attacks on Hawkesbury settlers were warranted and their ill-treatment of the Aborigines left a lot to be desired. Captain Paterson reported his concern for the natives stating there was 'no doubt of their having been cruelly treated by some of the first settlers'.

The first incident of Europeans being tried for murdering Aborigines took place in 1799 following the alleged murders of two teenage Aboriginal boys in the Hawkesbury district. Five men appeared in Court on trial and following four days of evidence and deliberation the prisoners were found guilty. Eventually a despatch from England in 1802 relayed the news that the five men charged with murder were acquitted. It was conveyed that the natives were, in the future, to be treated as humanely as possible.

In 1803 a settler from Portland Head on the Hawkesbury River presented a petition signed by many settlers in the area to Governor King requesting permission to shoot any natives on their farms. The petition proved to be a forgery and the man responsible was gaoled for several days. King sent for several Aborigines from that district and interviewed them. The natives stated 'they did not like to be driven from the few places that were left on the banks of the river, where ... they could procure food'. King agreed that their claim was fair and guaranteed not to settle any more grants lower down the river. The natives in return promised to be amicable. The conflicts gradually disappeared from the newspapers and official reports, possibly due to the introduction of rules and the fact that the Europeans maintained their authority with advanced weaponry.

During the 19th century the number of

A number of Aborigines worked for members of the Hall family at Lilburndale on the West Portland Road during the 19th century. (10.10.04 J. Auld)

Aborigines in the Hawkesbury dwindled and they either integrated and intermarried with Hawkesbury families or left the district. Some tried in vain to maintain their traditional way of life. Others lived on the fringes of European society and became reliant on the settlers for food and clothing. John Richmond, an Aborigine from Richmond, is recorded on a list in 1816 as receiving a grant of land at Pitt Town.

Some family groups worked on farms as labourers and were supplied rations as part of their wages. A number of Aborigines worked for the Hall family at Lilburndale on West Portland Road.

A surveyor named R. H. Mathews collected valuable information about the Aboriginal culture and language, including the Darug and Darkinung and one story relates to the Gu-ru-ngaty, a monster that lived on a lagoon near Sackville. Gu-ru-ngaty would drown and eat strangers. An important campsite was located on a creek between Windsor and Riverstone, near the junction of Eastern and South Creeks. Some camped on the property of Charles Marsden. The Kurrajong clan were living on the Bell property, Belmont at North Richmond.

One of the largest concentrations was around Sackville Reach and in 1889 the Minister of Lands, on behalf of the Aborigines of the district, proclaimed two reserves, one of 150 acres on Cumberland Reach and the other of 30 acres on Kent Reach. The larger of the two reserves was then named the Sackville Reach Aborigines Reserve. Four slab huts were built on the reserve in the 1890s and a church-meeting room was

An unnamed Aborigine on the Sackville Reach reserve in 1900.
(Copied by Jack Brook, HCCLS)

opened in 1900. It is believed there were other temporary buildings on the site during the early 1900s. There are various reports about the number of Aborigines that lived on the Reserve. In 1901, 50 Aborigines were recorded as living there.

At the turn of the century the *Windsor and Richmond Gazette* newspaper recorded that this 'Aboriginal Village' was an ideal system. The article stated that nearly all of the inhabitants were able to read and write and most played the violin or concertina. They had transport in the form of a horse and trap plus a government supplied boat. They used the boat to fish and sometimes peddled the excess catch around the town. The Aborigines from Sackville also worked as labourers on neighbouring farms, including Tizzana Winery at Sackville Reach. Many of the local Aborigines worked regularly at harvest with the Fiaschi's and held the family in high esteem. Some of the names associated with the Reserve include Barber, Everingham, Cox and Packer. Most of the children living on the Reserve had the opportunity to attend school. Students were transported by boat to Sackville Reach Public School but attendance was erratic.

Certain local Aborigines were renowned cricketers, many playing for local teams. A notable Aborigine to have lived and worked on Lilburndale at Sackville in the 1880s was the cricketer Tom Twopenny who was included in the first Australian cricket team (an all Aboriginal team) to tour England in 1868. Other prominent players included members of the Barber and Everingham families.

In 1926, the Sackville church register recorded the death of Martha Everingham aged 80, reported to be the last surviving full-blood Darug tribe member. The last Aborigine associated with the reserve, Andrew (Andy) Barber, died in 1943 and is buried in Windsor. Andy was born circa 1850 on the Lilburndale property. The reserve became a public reserve. In 1952 a stone obelisk was solemnly dedicated to the memory of the Hawkesbury Aborigines. An Aboriginal land claim in the early 1990s by the Daruk Land Council for Sackville Reserve was granted in 1993.

There are records of relationships between the early settlers and the local Aborigines. A number of local Aborigines married into or entered relationships with Hawkesbury families and have been researched by James Kohen and Jack Brooks. In the 1980s descendants of the Darug established a group called Darug Link to gather information about their extended families.

Within the Hawkesbury district approximately 200 Aboriginal sites have been recorded by the National Parks and Wildlife Service. The total number of sites is believed to be as many as 4000. Sensitive sites in the Hawkesbury local government area include rock shelters, open campsites and paintings.

During 2001 Centenary of Federation activities, the old bridge over Bardenarang Creek near Pitt Town was renamed Friendship Bridge and a sculpture of two hands clasped, was unveiled as an act of understanding and in memory of the original meeting between Governor Phillip, Yarramundi and the local Aborigines.

Hawesbury Aboriginal Cricket team, circa 1912. (HCCLS)

EXPLORATION & EUROPEAN SETTLEMENT

Three months after the arrival of the First Fleet Captain Arthur Phillip, on an expedition about 15 miles inland, had a good view of the mountains. One of these he named Richmond Hill in honour of Charles Lennox (1735-1806) Duke of Richmond. He was certain 'from the rising of these mountains ... that a large river would be found'. Shortly afterwards a party reached Prospect Hill, suitable for agricultural pursuits. Whilst examining the Broken Bay district Phillip sighted the mouth of the Hawkesbury and later returned on a second expedition. This journey successfully travelled the length of the Hawkesbury River and on the 6 July 1789 Phillip climbed Richmond Hill. He named the river after Lord Hawkesbury and reported on its fertile banks. The explorers cautiously noted that debris located 30 feet up in the trees indicated that the river flooded. Phillip also discovered the First or Lower Branch and the Second Branch of the river, which were later called the Macdonald and Colo Rivers respectively.

In 1791 Phillip, Tench, Hunter and others

GOVT HOUSE WINDSOR
N.S.WALES

ABOVE:
View of Thompson Square including the Doctors House at Windsor 1879. This area was originally the focus of commerce in the early 1800s and was named after Andrew Thompson. (GPO ML SLNSW)

OPPOSITE PAGE:
Government Cottage, George Street, Windsor 1879. It fell into disrepair in the 1900s and was demolished by 1919. (GPO ML SLNSW)

explored the Nepean and Hawkesbury Rivers. A second expedition the following month a party, including Tench, Dawes and Sergeant Knight, explored Richmond Hill to confirm whether it was situated on the Nepean or Hawkesbury Rivers. This excursion confirmed the Hawkesbury and Nepean were in fact the one river.

Captain Paterson of the NSW Corps led a group including Captain Johnston and Mr Palmer in 1793. They explored the base of the Blue Mountains and travelled about 10 miles further up the river than any others had, and named the Grose River. Paterson, also a botanist, collected some plants and tested the soil.

By early 1794 a group of 22 settlers were allowed to select 25 to 30 acre farms along the Hawkesbury River and South Creek tributary. Lieutenant-Governor Major Grose reported in an official despatch in 1794 that the settlers 'seem very much pleased with their farms. They describe the soil as particularly rich, and they inform me whatever they have planted has grown in the greatest luxuriance'. The exact date of commencement is not known but in January 1794 David Collins recorded in his memoirs *An Account of the English Colony in NSW* that another group of settlers was 'added to the list of those already established.' It stated that these settlers 'chose for themselves allotments of ground conveniently situated for fresh water, and not

OPPOSITE PAGE ABOVE:
The old Windsor Hospital Macquarie Street, Windsor 1879, was originally established as Convict Barracks in 1820 and converted to a Hospital in 1823.
(GPO ML SLNSW)

LEFT:
Windsor Courthouse was designed by Francis Greenway and built by William Cox in 1822. Justice has been dispensed from the 1820s and the courthouse is still in use today.
(GPO ML SLNSW)

OPPOSITE PAGE BELOW:
Richmond Park 1879 was originally marked as a market square, hence the street names East Market and West Market Streets.
(GPO ML SLNSW)

much burdened with timber'. This early settlement was located between Pitt Reach on the Hawkesbury River and South Creek tributary and the fertile plains rapidly produced crops. The area became known as the Green Hills. The term Mulgrave Place was used to describe the surrounding Hawkesbury district. The river provided a link between the settlements, establishing vital communications with Parramatta and Sydney. The food produced at the Hawkesbury allowed the colony to stabilise and it was described as 'the granary of the colony.'

The small community was very isolated and a track linking it to Sydney was completed by mid 1794. It only took about eight hours to walk and the area expanded with more grants. Within two years of settlement, 3955 acres were granted in the Hawkesbury to 135 persons.

There were numerous explorations by Phillip, Tench, Dawes, Hacking, Bass, Barrallier and Caley. In 1795 ex-convict and local settler Matthew Everingham set out to explore a route over the Blue Mountains. He decided to follow the ridges and the party reputedly made it to Kurrajong Heights but then discarded the 'Ridge' plan and forged ahead. They got as far as Mount Tomah or Mount Irvine. George Caley in 1804 traversed the Kurrajong area and Mount Tomah and he named Mount Banks.

A detachment of two officers and 60 privates of the NSW Corps were dispatched to the Green Hills in 1795 after several skirmishes between the Aborigines and the settlers. Paterson, who had taken over after Grose left the colony, justified his actions as he 'very much feared they [the settlers] would have abandoned the settlement entirely and given up the most fertile spot which had been discovered in the colony'. By 1799 temporary barracks were built. Other public buildings were established under Governor Hunter including accommodation for the commanding officer of the military. A weatherboard Government Cottage was built and used by visiting officials.

Elizabeth, the wife of John Macarthur, visited the Hawkesbury district in 1795 and observed that the 'soil in the valley of this river is most productive, and greatly superior to any that has been tilled in this country.' The centre of settlement focused around the north end of Windsor close to the wharf and Bell Post Square. By 1799, 55 per cent of the cultivated land in the colony was in the Hawkesbury, 37 per cent at Parramatta and 14 per cent at Sydney.

During the early years of settlement of the Hawkesbury, the inhabitants were recorded as unruly and reckless although some settlers were keeping their heads down and toiling away. The Hawkesbury district was far from Sydney's administrative control and social attitudes were lax with the majority of the population being emancipated convicts. Philip Gidley King appointed Charles Grimes who was the deputy surveyor and lived in the district, as magistrate in 1800 to bring some order to the far-flung community.

MACQUARIE'S FIVE TOWNS

Governor Lachlan Macquarie arrived in the closing months of 1809 with orders to bring order and harmony to the colony. The settlement had experienced several years of turbulence including the Rum Rebellion and the unsettled rule of Governor William Bligh.

Lachlan Macquarie was born in Ulva in Scotland in 1761. When he was 15 years old he joined the British army, serving in the American colonies and India, rising through the ranks. He served in Egypt and India, returning briefly to Britain in 1807 to wed a distant relative Elizabeth Henrietta Campbell, his second wife. Macquarie had been promoted to Lieutenant-Colonel of the 73rd Regiment in 1805 and in 1809 was selected to replace William Bligh as the Governor of NSW. Macquarie commenced his period in office in 1810.

Under his influence the colony prospered. His humanitarian vision of a free community, his public works agenda and the building of barracks and hospitals, his concern for public morality, roadworks, the re-admission of ex-convicts to society, establishing a coinage and the first bank, were all stabilising acts.

Macquarie created several new positions including Andrew Thompson as the Hawkesbury's Justice of the Peace and magistrate. He provided government-funded boats to freight the grain from the Hawkesbury to the Sydney markets, which was welcomed by local farmers. He also toured the district, and travelled further afield in New South Wales and Van Diemen's Land. He encouraged exploration.

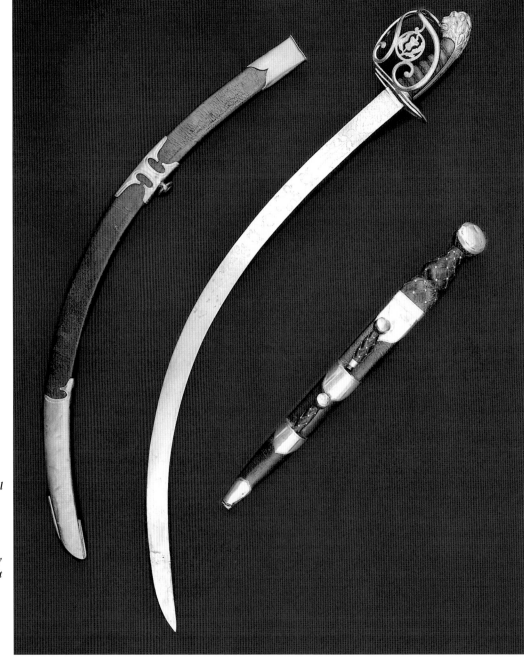

The ceremonial sword of Governor Lachlan Macquarie is now on display in Government House, Sydney. (National Museum of Australia)

TOUR TO THE HAWKESBURY

After touring the Nepean district, Macquarie arrived in the Hawkesbury. He viewed the Grose River and camped at Yarramundi Lagoon. In early December the party explored Richmond Hill, Kurrajong and Richmond Terrace by horseback. They also visited Mrs Bell, wife of Lieutenant Archibald Bell at North Richmond. Macquarie kept a journal of his tour and noted that they '... rode through a fine open Forest and Hilly Country for about 5 miles to the Foot of the Curry [sic] Jung Hill, which is very long and steep to ascend, arriving on the summit ... and from whence we had a very grand noble Prospect of the low grounds on both Banks of the River Hawkesbury as far as the Green Hills ...'. They travelled via The Terrace and crossed the Hawkesbury River near Windsor by ferry. The night was spent at Government Cottage at the Green Hills. Macquarie wrote: 'Mrs. M. and myself were quite delighted with the beauty of this part of the Country; its great fertility, and its Picturesque appearance'.

Macquarie attended a church service at the Green Hills then travelled by carriage to the 'new Burying Ground ... to view the Tomb where the remains of our late worthy and highly esteemed good friend Mr. Andw. Thompson, late Chief Magistrate of this District, are deposited, and whose loss we both very sincerely lament and

ABOVE:
The portrait of Governor Lachlan Macquarie that hangs in Windsor Courthouse.
(HCCLS)

RIGHT:
The Settlement on the Green Hills, Hawkesbury River, NSW 1809, *a watercolour attributed to George William Evans.*
(ML SLNSW)

deplore, and from whose superior local knowledge and good sound sense and judicious advice [we are missing]'. They then visited some of Thompson's property, West Hill (or Red House Farm) and Killarney.

The following day Macquarie surveyed the grounds for the site of Richmond township. He observed an assortment of farms noting the rich soil and the fine crops. He noticed 'the Houses and Habitations of the Settlers are miserably bad' and that most of the farms were prone to flooding. The party explored the Hawkesbury River as far as Portland Head and were impressed with the farms and orchards. They travelled by carriage from Dr Arndell's farm through the Nelson District and examined the site for a township. On Thursday 6 December 1810, a large social gathering was held at the Government Cottage and Macquarie noted

After Dinner I christened the new Townships, drinking a Bumper to the success of each. I gave the name of Windsor to the Town intended to be erected in the District of the Green Hills, in continuation of the present Village, from the similarity of this situation to that of the same name in England; the Township in the Richmond District I have named Richmond, from its beautiful situation, and as corresponding with that of its District; the Township for the Evan or Nepean District I have named Castlereagh in honor of Lord Viscount Castlereagh; the Township of the Nelson District I have named Pitt-Town in honor of the immortal memory of the late great William Pitt, the Minister who originally planned this Colony; and the Township for the Phillip District; on the North or left Bank of the Hawkesbury, I have named Wilberforce — in honor of and out of respect to the good and virtuous Wm. Wilberforce Esqr. M.P. — a true Patriot and the

real Friend of Mankind. Having sufficiently celebrated this auspicious Day of christening the five Towns and Townships, intended to be erected and established for the security and accommodation of the Settlers and others inhabiting the Cultivated Country, on the Banks of the Rivers Hawkesbury and Nepean; I recommended to the Gentlemen present to exert their influence with the Settlers in stimulating them to lose no time in removing their Habitations, Flocks and Herds to these Places of safety and security, and thereby fulfil my intentions and plans in establishing them.

Macquarie wanted the settlers to waste no time in moving to higher ground. He appreciated the importance of the fertile Hawkesbury floodplains and he did not want to vacate the area entirely.

Explorers Blaxland, Wentworth and Lawson found a successful route across the Blue Mountains in 1813 and productive, flood-free lands in the west. George Evans surveyed a route over the mountains and William Cox constructed a road by 1815. The Hawkesbury still played a major role supplying produce to Sydney

There were several efforts to find a route through to the Hunter Valley from the Hawkesbury. William Parr and Benjamin Singleton made an attempt in 1817, Benjamin Singleton again in 1818, but it was John Howe accompanied by Benjamin Singleton who found a route in 1819. Howe with Singleton and Myles, a local Aboriginal guide, negotiated a quicker route that became the stock route. The locality of Singleton, where he was later granted land, bears Benjamin's name whilst Howe Creek and Valley acquired John's name.

Under Macquarie's leadership the colony, including the Hawkesbury flourished. Townships were surveyed with streets, reserves and building

sites being carefully marked. There was an influx of convicts who were quickly absorbed into the large public works agenda. Many local buildings were completed at this time with some surviving today.

Conflict arose with the self-styled ruling class who were not fond of Macquarie's lenient policies regarding convicts and emancipists. Despite his integrity and fairness some of the influential members of society instigated political pressure that ultimately led to a Commission of Inquiry into the state of affairs of the colony led by the officious J. T. Bigge. Bigge reported on the transportation system, legal system plus the state of agriculture and the economy. Disheartened Macquarie had tendered his resignation several times before it was eventually accepted and he returned to England in 1822.

Prior to his departure, Macquarie visited the Hawkesbury district with Sir Thomas Brisbane. They inspected the new St Matthew's Church as well as other public buildings in Windsor. The Hawkesbury inhabitants presented Macquarie with an Address which commended him on all aspects of his administration. They requested Macquarie sit for a portrait which they would hang in the Court House and it has hung there since 1822. Major General Lachlan Macquarie died in London in 1824 and is buried on his estate on Mull off the coast of Scotland.

In 1994 the Hawkesbury celebrated 200 years of European settlement with a Pioneer's Day, parade and tree planting. A monument was erected in memory of Lachlan Macquarie in McQuade Park. The statue was created by Frederic Chepeaux, a French born sculptor who unfortunately died prior to the unveiling of the statue by the then Governor of NSW, his Excellency Rear Admiral Peter Sinclair AC.

St Matthew's Anglican Church, Windsor 1879, was designed by Francis Greenway the convict Macquarie appointed civil architect. (GPO ML SLNSW)

HAWKESBURY LOCALITIES

Agnes Banks

Andrew Thompson was a prosperous ex-convict who arrived on the *Pitt* in 1792. He made use of the opportunities available to emancipated convicts and accumulated a large fortune. He was Chief Constable, magistrate, farmer and a businessman involved in brewing and shipping activities. He made the Hawkesbury his home in 1796 and most of his businesses were centred in the district. He purchased much land and was granted a lease of one acre at the Green Hills in 1799. Thompson Square, the oldest public square in Australia, bears his name. During 1804 Governor King granted Thompson 278 acres along the Nepean River which he named Agnes Banks in memory of his mother. Agnes Banks is located on the outskirts of Richmond, near Yarramundi.

Thompson concerned himself in flood rescues in the early 1800s which regrettably affected his health and led to his premature death in 1810 aged 37 years. He left a quarter of his large estate to his friend, Governor Lachlan Macquarie who in turn erected the monument in his memory at St Matthew's Anglican Cemetery.

ABOVE:
Osborne at Agnes Banks in the 1960s was named by Ronald Barr, the property owner from 1926 to 1980s. (HCCLS)

RIGHT:
Tyreel has operated as a horse stud for many years. (HCCLS)

Following Thompson's death the estate was put up for sale but did not sell until 1815 when John Campbell, Macquarie's secretary purchased it as an investment. Houses were established on the property by 1823. The *Sydney Gazette* described two farmhouses plus 'the largest and best peachery in full bearing ever planted in the colony'. The property came into the ownership of the Williams family in 1839 and was later subdivided.

Tyreel is one of several prestigious horse studs. The property was purchased by John Williams from family in 1879 and named Tyreel after a property he owned in Moree. Williams constructed the current house in 1880. There is a lovely garden with a number of grand old trees including a magnolia tree over 100 years old.

There are other historic buildings at Agnes Banks. Bronte homestead is on the Castlereagh Road. Bronte was one of the original properties granted to the Matcham Pitt family. The old schoolhouse is another notable building. A local school operated from 1875 until 1908 and from 1923 until it was closed in 1970. Known as Yarramundi School until 1923 and then as Agnes Banks School, it is now a residence.

Several churches were at Agnes Banks including St Paul's Anglican. This weatherboard church was relocated to the University of Western Sydney Richmond campus in 1991. Another brick church was built on land donated by Henry Farlow on the understanding it was to be used by any denomination. It was demolished in the 1970s.

Early settlers are remembered in street names. Samuel Freeman was a convict who was given his emancipation in return for his work as a carpenter on the first road over the Blue Mountains with William Cox. He worked as a millwright at Agnes Banks. Price Street remembers Edward Price who arrived in 1791 and was a carpenter in the district.

There are large amounts of sand deposited in this vicinity and these deposits have been removed over the last 50 years for the purpose of bricklaying, concrete industry and the manufacture of special sands for the glass industry.

The first Australian feature film with sound was *On our Selection* which opened in 1932. The outdoor location scenes were filmed at Castlereagh and Agnes Banks.

Berambing

Berambing is located about 6 kilometres south west of Bilpin. George Meares Countess Bowen (1803-1889) arrived in Australia in 1827. He received a 2560 acre land grant at what is known today as Berambing. The grant was authorised in 1829 and he moved there some time later. He named the property Bulgamatta which translated from Aboriginal is a mixture of 'mountain' and 'water'.

The property was covered with timber and his

Hungerford children at their home Burando, Berambing, in the 1930s. (Molly Brown)

Clarence Hungerford robbing the beehive at Berambing in the 1940s. (BC HCCLS)

reaction to the clearing of this primitive land was emotive, '… sentiment must yield to the rough business of life … the axes were plied, the chips flew about, and presently the lords of the forest toppled and fell, crash succeeded crash, until the hideous ruin strewed the ground'.

He cleared some of the property and constructed a home but sold Bulgamatta in 1836 due to its isolation. Captain Robert Town purchased it for £600 and it was managed by Samuel Senior. The other veterans did not stay long in the area and their grants were sold during the 1840s.

Archibald and Martha Kennedy and their family lived at Berambing during the 1870s. Tragedy struck the family and several children died due to an epidemic, and oral history records they are buried near the boundary of the property. Towards the end of the 19th century more families moved into the Berambing area. Residents in the 1930s included the Stringer, Hambly, Entwistle and Hungerford families. Clarence Hungerford (1895-1958) lived at Berambing for many years. He conducted a sawmill and was also involved in the development of the honey industry. 'Old Tamar' was also used in the 19th century to describe Berambing.

Berambing is also the mythical place in the *Longtime Passing* books written by author Hesba Brinsmead. Hesba Fay Hungerford (1922-2003) was born at Berambing. Her home was located in a small clearing with no electricity or running water. The road to their house was a bullock track. With a childhood in the wilderness, she wrote the 'Longtime' series, a semi-autobiographical trilogy set in Berambing. In this story she describes the beauty of the bushland and the early history and the struggles of the Aboriginal past. She won the Children's Book of the Year Award in 1971.

Bilpin

The village of Bilpin is situated along the Bells Line of Road about 25 kilometres from the North Richmond bridge. The name Bilpin was in use by the early 1830s but there is no record of its meaning. During the 1830s, discharged Royal Veterans were offered land grants in the vicinity of Bilpin. Some took up the grants but did not stay long and the allotments were left empty by 1839. They were auctioned in the 1840s. One of the earliest landowners was the Howells who built a log house and established an orchard, with a caretaker looking after the property. By the 1870s, McEwan, a drover with resting paddocks, James McCauley and Mr Wilson are mentioned as living in the village.

By the 1890s residents included the Williamsons and the Pecks and Gillman Norwood who, as well as running the orchard, managed the local post office from 1899 on his property Norwood. This is why Bilpin was sometimes confusingly called Norwood. Mail was incorrectly sent to Norwood in South Australia until the post office reverted to the name Bilpin in 1914. The locality known as Tabarag is located along the Bells Line of Road about 15 kilometres from the North Richmond bridge and includes Glenara and Pittmans Road.

Clem Pittman (1869-1952) who came from a Kurrajong family settled at Bilpin and built

ABOVE:
Ferngrove the Bullock home in Bilpin built circa 1910.
(BC HCCLS)

RIGHT:
Hanlon's transport truck in front of Hanlon's store at Bilpin in 1942. (BC HCCLS)

Washing day under the grass trees at Fernleigh circa 1910. (BC HCCLS)

Weeroona in 1912. He married in 1915. Alfred Slingsby Snr, with wife Gertrude and family moved to Bilpin around the turn of the century. They were originally from Blaxlands Ridge. Their home was called Fernleigh and Alfred is attributed with cultivating the first Jonathan apples in Bilpin.

Peter Powell grew apples and oranges. Around 1913, he constructed a packing shed, popular on Saturday nights for local dances. Henry Bullock Snr acquired land at Bilpin. In his early years, he worked at Andrew Town's Hobartville as a groom. He married Charlotte Travis who was also employed at Hobartville. Henry Snr conveyed some of his land to his son Harry who married Beatrice Slingsby. They lived in their new home Ferngrove. It is understood Harry Bullock was the first to drive a motor car from Bilpin to Bell in 1913.

The Hanlon family arrived in Bilpin about 1912. Michael Hanlon purchased the Slingsby property and he managed the orchard and grew passionfruits. His son Jack established a boarding house called Allegro and commenced a transport business taking fruit to Richmond Railway and later to Kurrajong, when the line was extended. He also started a grocery store in 1929 which had a petrol bowser. Hanlon's trucks carried apples and timber. The store is still run by family members. Peter's sister Florence Powell ran a subsidised school from about 1910. A provisional school operated from 1927 then Bilpin Public School was established in 1952.

A School of Arts was established in 1909, which was used for concerts, dances and a public hall. The hall was replaced in 1948 and the name was changed to Memorial Hall, in memory of local soldiers. A third hall was constructed in 1967 and named Bilpin District Hall. The hall is used for a variety of purposes including regular markets and flower shows.

Blaxlands Ridge

Five years after the discovery of the new track to the Hunter Valley in 1820, John M. Blaxland, a settler living near Broke, wrote to the Surveyor General to say he had discovered a shorter route. Blaxland was the son of Gregory Blaxland the explorer. This new route went along Comleroy Road then followed what is now Blaxlands Ridge, crossed the Colo River near Morans Rock, ascended Colo Heights and turned east along Wheelbarrow Ridge, then onto Wollombi. The road was not built but Blaxland's name was used for the ridge.

Blaxlands Ridge is one of a number of ridges in the Kurrajong district where communities settled. By the 1890s there were a number of orchards producing apples, oranges, stone fruit and grapes. Some of the early families included Tierney, Overton, Slingsby, Wholohan, Horney and McCabe. A provisional school commenced at Blaxlands Ridge in 1892 and was upgraded and became Blaxlands Ridge Public School in 1906, closing in 1977. The first teacher was Miss Edith Black and she is remembered by the naming of a street. One of the longest serving teachers was Miss Amelia Honora 'Nora' Connor who taught at the school between 1928 and 1947.

Originally the home of James and Elizabeth Overton at Blaxland Ridge, this house was sold to the Hennessys. (Coral Cleary)

Bligh Park and Windsor Downs

In 1982, the NSW State Government in a joint venture with Hawkesbury Council, released about 200 hectares of Crown Land for urban development. This land was known as the Rifle Range and Temporary Common. Bounded by Rifle Range Road, the land was subdivided and the development subsequently named Bligh Park in memory of Governor William Bligh (1754-1817). Many of the streets throughout Bligh Park, as suggested by Hawkesbury Historical Society, were named for the early Hawkesbury pioneers and ships of the First Fleet.

Bligh, renowned for the infamous *Bounty* incident, arrived in Australia as Governor in 1806. He had aimed to suppress the military monopoly and this made him unpopular with the NSW Corps. He was admired by the Hawkesbury settlers. In 1808, John Macarthur and some members of the NSW Corps deposed Bligh and put him under house arrest. Major George Johnston became Lieutenant-Governor followed by Major Joseph Foveaux then Colonel William Paterson until Colonel Lachlan Macquarie arrived and commenced duties in 1810. Bligh returned to England to face a court hearing where Johnston ended up being court-martialled and Bligh cleared of any offences.

A more recent development Windsor Downs, was originally part of the Riverstone Meatworks and owned by the Angliss Meat Company. The grazing land was re-zoned as rural residential blocks and made available for sale in 1990.

Windsor Downs Nature Reserve is made up of 332 hectares of Cumberland Plain woodland vegetation. The reserve was originally part of Richard Rouse's Jericho Farm grant, that became part of the Riverstone Meatworks.

Bligh Park in the early stages of development in the 1980s. (RAAF)

Bowen Mountain

Named after George Meares Countess Bowen (1803-1889) who graduated from Sandhurst then following service in India, Galway and the Channel Islands he arrived in Australia in 1827 as a lieutenant in the 39th regiment. He was employed in the surveyor-general's office in Sydney and later became land commissioner. Bowen had a grant at Bulgamatta near Mt Tomah between 1831 and 1836, when he sold the land.

He travelled overseas between 1843-46 and on his return to Australia Bowen acquired substantial land holdings throughout the Kurrajong region, including Burralow Creek valley. He also purchased a number of properties along the adjacent ridge known today as Bowen Mountain and lived there quietly.

ABOVE: Castlereagh school in the 1970s. (HCCLS)

View along Bowen Mountain Road, 1960s. (HCCLS)

Castlereagh

Castlereagh is located on the road between Richmond and Penrith on the Nepean River flood plain, rich with alluvial soil. Castlereagh Road linked the Nepean district with the Hawkesbury. The first grants were made in 1803, with additional grants the following year. Today's Castlereagh is 5 kilometres from the site chosen by Macquarie.

In 1810 Governor Macquarie visited the Hawkesbury and named five new towns. He was optimistic that these would develop into fine urban settlements and be places of safety and prosperity. This township he named after Lord Viscount Castlereagh. Depite further grants, Castlereagh did not develop and the main focus of the district was Penrith, formerly known as Evan.

The land on which the first Wesleyan Church in Australia was built was part of a grant to John

Lees in 1804. In 1817, the small chapel was opened, replaced in 1848 with the present church and is now run by the Uniting Church as a retreat. The cemetery dates from 1836.

Christ Church was established in Church Lane and consecrated in 1878 after an earlier building was destroyed by fire. Some fine examples of early rural buildings survive at Castlereagh including Nepean House and Hadley Park. In 1895 the Municipality of Castlereagh was proclaimed and operated until 1948.

Penrith Lakes Scheme commenced in the 1980s when several large quarrying companies combined forces. Today this area supplies over half of Sydney's sand and gravel materials. Ongoing development has regrettably had a huge impact on the charming Castlereagh village and its surrounds. Despite much debate and community agitation over the proposal fertile rural farms and significant heritage items will be lost. At present, the Lakes Scheme consists of the International Regatta Centre, various lakes, parklands and historic sites.

Cattai

Cattai is the name of the Aboriginal group who lived in the area. Caddie Park was the name used by Thomas Arndell (1753-1821) who arrived with the First Fleet as the assistant-surgeon, to describe his 600 acre grant on the banks of the Hawkesbury. Descendants of the Arndell family lived and farmed on this property until 1981 when it was purchased by the National Parks & Wildlife Service. In 1952 enterprising members of the family opened the property for picnics, camping and water skiing. Caddie Park including the homestead built in 1821, Hope Farm and Mitchell Park are now known as Cattai National Park. Mitchell Park was originally part of the Pitt Town Common and has long been used as a recreational area.

George Hall, one of the 1802 *Coromandel* settlers was granted land at Cattai in 1803. His descendants called the property Bungool and it passed out of family hands in 1912. In the 1960s it was used as picnic and water ski grounds. In the 1970s it was purchased by Paradise Gardens as a pleasure park and was known for its concrete dinosaurs. Riverside Oaks is now located on this site.

Cattai Creek was a popular recreation venue in the 19th and 20th century. (HCCLS)

Clarendon

Clarendon is half way between Windsor and Richmond. It takes its name from William Cox's property. The name for the locality of Clarendon was in use by 1811. William Cox (1764–1837) was an enterprising pioneer of the Hawkesbury. He arrived with his family on the *Minerva* in 1800 as paymaster for the NSW Corps. He was involved in the construction of major buildings such as the courthouse and rectory at Windsor as well as his properties, Hobartville at Richmond and Fairfield in Windsor, all of which

still stand. He was appointed as the chief magistrate following the death of Andrew Thompson in 1810. He is recognised for the construction of the road over the Blue Mountains from Emu Plains to Bathurst, which commenced in 1814. Involved in many community activities, he was popular with the inhabitants of the Hawkesbury. He built Clarendon in the early 1800s, situated on Dight Street at the back of the RAAF Base. The estate was described in the 1820s as 'the seat of Mr Cox, that veteran Justice of the Peace, is situated in a pretty spot and presents the appearance of a small town' as he had set up a

number of manufacturing projects including a tannery and woollen cloth factory with two looms.

When Cox moved to Windsor in 1834 he leased Clarendon to Laban White. The house was leased to others before being sold to the Dight family and then to Philip Charley in 1909 for £7,500. The old house became uninhabitable around the 1900s and by 1911 was described as being in ruins. The servant's quarters and some outbuildings have survived.

There have been several hotels at Clarendon. The old two storey building butting onto the

Clarendon village and railway station in the 1920s. (HCCLS)

LEFT:
Richmond RAAF Base in 1927.
(HCCLS)

OPPOSITE PAGE ABOVE:
Charles Kingsford Smith (left) at Richmond RAAF Base in the late 1920s.
(HCCLS)

OPPOSITE PAGE BELOW:
Wally Shiers, Frank Hurley, Keith Smith and Jim Bennett with camera equipment alongside the Vickers Vimy. Thousands of onlookers visited the plane whilst it was housed at Richmond in 1920.
(HCCLS)

BELOW:
Richmond RAAF No. 5 Squadron 1936. (HCCLS)

RAAF Base and now operating as a bed and breakfast facility was once known as the Bird in Hand. William Thomas Baylis(s) was a farmer as well as publican, holding the licence for this hotel from 1834 to 1840. Alfred Smith ran the Butchers Arms for about four years. Smith recalls the accidental death of Richard Lewis who lived near the Clarendon railway station and had been into Windsor on business. He fell off his horse on the way home and landed unconscious on a 'big red ants nest. When he was found he was all but stung to death'. The Aerodrome Hotel was established in 1938 but a fire destroyed it in the 1980s.

An extension of the Blacktown-Richmond railway line was opened in 1864 with stations at Riverstone, Mulgrave, Windsor and Richmond. When a racecourse was established at Clarendon in 1871 the need for public transport grew and a platform called Racecourse was opened. It was renamed Clarendon in 1876 and the Hawkesbury Racecourse platform was built opposite in 1889.

In 1879 the Hawkesbury District Agricultural Association (HDAA) was established with the support of the whole community including prominent landowners. The following year an agricultural show was organised and this annual three-day event still takes place today. Shows were based on agricultural activities, livestock and produce, and flowers, wines, fine arts and agricultural implements were exhibited along with the popular ploughing contests. Idiosyncratic contests include the apple and water race, corn husking, sheaf tossing, sleeper squaring, tug-o-war, wood chopping and more recently motorcycle races and tractor driving. There have been boxing and wrestling proceedings as well as snake charmers and sensational sideshow acts. Originally, the shows were held at the Hawkesbury Race Club but in the 1990s the HDAA acquired land

of its own at Clarendon and the Hawkesbury Show continues as an important annual community event.

Regular races were held throughout the Hawkesbury district particularly at McGraths Hill and Clarendon and there have been a number of racecourses throughout the area. Hawkesbury Race Club was officially established in 1829 and is one of the oldest race clubs in existence in Australia. In 1865 Crown Land was leased to the Club and a grandstand and racetrack built. The first Hawkesbury Grand Handicap was run in 1871 with a purse of 120 sovereigns. Today the racetrack at Clarendon has been rejuvenated with new buildings and on major race days it is one of the state's leading tracks.

In 1911 aviator, William Ewart Hart, a dentist from Parramatta purchased a Bristol aeroplane and obtained the first Australian pilot's licence. Hart moved his plane to Ham Common on the outskirts of Richmond and set up an airfield the following year. Unfortunately Hart crashed a plane that was built at Richmond and he was out of action for several years. During World War I a flying school was established at Clarendon by Frenchman Maurice Guillaux, followed by fellow citizen Marduel, but they returned to France. In 1915 the NSW Government set up the NSW

ABOVE:
Early aviation at Clarendon. (HCCLS)

LEFT:
WAAAF servicing an Anson in 1942. (RAAF)

Flying School at Clarendon to provide pilots for the Australian Flying Corps. Land was reclaimed on Ham Common for aviation purposes in 1916. The first trainers were Billy Stutt and Andrew Lang, both experienced with military flying in England. The site was in use until the end of World War I.

The Royal Australian Air Force (RAAF) was established in 1921 and two years later acquired the site at Clarendon and established the second airbase in Australia. During World War II, the RAAF stationed at Richmond prepared paratroopers and carried out training. In 1941 the Women's Auxiliary Australian Air Force (WAAAF) was formed and many women were housed at the base.

Following World War II the RAAF intensified work in military aviation transport. In the late 1950s the first of the Hercules appeared at Richmond and these, and subsequent newer models, aided the moving of troops and cargo during training sessions and conflicts. The Hercules has also been used during disasters such as Cyclone Tracy, East Timor and the Bali bombing. These days the main function of the RAAF base is to support the Australian Defence Force and United Nations sponsored tasks.

They also conduct medical evacuations and search and rescue manoeuvres.

Charles Kingsford-Smith was often seen landing and taking off at the airfield. He housed the Southern Cross in a hangar at the base. Charles Ulm and Kingsford-Smith flew the first trans-Pacific flight from America to Australia and arrived in Richmond in 1928. The first trans-Tasman flight to New Zealand departed from Richmond in 1928, and locals packed the airfield to witness the event. The first female to land at Clarendon was Amy Johnson, the first woman to fly solo from England to Australia, arriving in 1930. New Zealand born Jean Batten, who made several record-breaking flights also used the airfield at Clarendon.

RIGHT:
The Hawkesbury show in 1929. (HCCLS)

Colo

The catchment area of the Colo River and its tributaries is about 5000 square kilometres. It makes up almost half of the Greater Blue Mountains World Heritage area. The Colo River includes a section called the Colo Gorge that is 30 kilometres and 300 metres deep, apparently the longest gorge in Australia.

Governor Phillip, Captain Hunter and their party were the first Europeans to visit the Colo area when they were exploring the Hawkesbury River in 1789. They named the river the 'Second Branch'. The group noted the 'high, steep and rocky mountains'. The Colo Valley was explored when Parr, Singleton and Howe journeyed through the area in search of a route north. Howe mentions the Colo River as early as 1819.

The Colo River Valley's ruggedness and isolation made the area unattractive to all but resilient settlers. Grants were made at the confluence of the Colo and Hawkesbury River in the early 1800s. In 1804, grants were recorded as being issued to William McDonald, James Sherwin, William Yarley, Peter Hibbs and his son George. Further grants were promised yet not authorized until the 1830s when the area had been officially surveyed. In 1823, more grants were made to settlers including John Cribb, James Cavanough and James Turnbull, Thomas Gosper Snr and sons John, Joseph and James. Another family with lengthy connections to the Colo is the McDougall family. Andrew and Elizabeth McDougall with sons Andrew, James and John arrived as free settlers from Scotland in 1798. They are recorded as living on the Colo by 1818 and descendants are still living there today. Other settlers were the Law, Blundell, Christie, Manning, Eather, Hulbert, Miller and Reynolds families. A later arrival was the Ward family who settled at Upper Colo in the early 1900s. Many of the Ward descendants are still living in the area.

In the late 1850s Robert Coffin lived for 12 months in the Colo Valley working for Charles Ivory. Coffin was an American seaman on his way to the goldfields who later published his memoirs. Coffin wrote about the isolation in the Colo as well as the difficulties of transporting supplies. Most goods went in and out of the valley by riverboat. Roads followed the tops of the ridges but some of the peaks were too steep for wheeled vehicles and goods had to be carried up and down.

There were two public wharves as well as private ones. From the 1860s a punt crossed at Lower Portland near the mouth of the Colo. It was replaced in the 1970s by a bridge. By 1910 the residents of the Colo everyday needs were supplied by floating store boats such as the *Camac*.

George Cavanough married Jane Gosper in 1836 in Windsor and they moved to the Upper Colo where Jane's parents lived and built a weatherboard house, also used as a boarding house. Located almost opposite the current church on the rise of the hill it was a popular overnight stay as the Comleroy Road was a busy thoroughfare. The house was used for community gatherings including dances and may also have

*SS **Hawkesbury** and SS **Narara** at the junction of the Colo and Hawkesbury Rivers in 1904. (HCCLS)*

A Wesleyan Chapel was also established in the Colo district but destroyed by the 1867 flood.

The main businesses in the Colo Valley were mixed farming, fruit growing and raising stock, with corn and oranges being popular. Timber was cut in the 19th century and used for a house and boat building. John Duffy operated a sawmill from 1929 at Upper Colo. Timber cutters also supplied vast numbers of railway sleepers from this area in the early 1900s.

Wollemi National Park covers more than 500 000 hectares and is the largest wilderness area in NSW. The diverse environment is home to significant plant communities and in 1994 the Wollemi Pine was discovered inside the park. In 2003 a rare gallery of 203 Aboriginal drawings were discovered, some up to 4000 years old.

A view of the Anglican Church and the Cavanough cottage in the Upper Colo. (HCCLS)

been used as a licensed inn although there is no official proof.

Spencer Eather (1906-1972) was an orchardist and mailman in the Colo. His delivery route was Upper Colo to Lower Portland via Wheeny Creek in the 1930s. Three times a week he would ride his bike from Central Colo to Upper Colo to pick up the mail from the post office, then return to Central Colo to pick up his horse and the sulky to deliver to Lower Portland. He also carried groceries, passengers and mail, and cut hair, at no charge.

In 1857 the Gosper family donated land to build an Anglican church and burial ground at Upper Colo. From the late 1850s a building had been used as a combined church and school. A church was informally opened on this site in 1906 and about 200 persons attended the celebrations.

A party travelling up the road to Colo. (HCCLS)

Comleroy Road

Northwest of Kurrajong, one of the oldest settlements in the area was along Comleroy Road. From about 1819 this was the main route to the Hunter Valley used to drive cattle. The name Comleroy is supposedly derived from the Kamilaroi tribe that inhabited part of this region.

William Parr managed an expedition from the site of Singleton's Mill near Wheeny Creek at Kurrajong in 1817 looking for a route north. Benjamin Singleton accompanied him and tried again in 1818. It was John Howe who found the first northern route in 1819. It was known as Howe's Track or the Bulga Road. Little more than a bridle track, it was used to move stock. It was also used by escaped convicts and cattle thieves. In 1823 a permit was required for persons and stock to travel the road. The Great North Road superseded this road although it was still used by drovers and stock until well after the turn of the century. Flocks of 10 000 sheep were being driven along the Bulga Road but by the 1920s the numbers had faded to nothing as stock was moved by rail or truck. There was renewed interest in the road during World War II when an alternate route to the coast was needed and it was completed in by 1942. The Singleton or Putty Road links Wilberforce with the Hunter via the old road through Howes Valley and Bulga.

Some of the early settlers in this district were the John, Eather, Ezzey, Peck and Dargin families who engaged in mixed farming and fruit and vegetable growing. John and Mary McMahon arrived as free settlers from Ireland in 1839, soon making their way to the Hawkesbury. Their sons and daughters settled around this area and descendants still live here. William Freeman lived along Comleroy Road and conducted a public house known as The Travellers Rest in the early 1800s. This was later sold to Michael McMahon who established his Garryowen property.

A Wesleyan chapel was established on Comleroy Road in 1854, but later replaced. It was destroyed in the December 1944 bushfires and not rebuilt. The small adjacent cemetery still survives. A timber church was relocated to the corner of Comleroy and Single Ridge Roads in 1908, with

The moving of the church at Comleroy in 1908 by bullock dray. (HCCLS)

the assistance of 35 bullocks and a specially designed sledge. The *Windsor and Richmond Gazette* newspaper reported there was a 'large crowd of people, numbering some hundreds, followed the operations throughout, and had the affair been known more widely the attendance would have been more than doubled'. This building was burned down in the devastating bushfires in 1944 but rebuilt and opened in 1946.

A public school was established in 1880 and the Comleroy Road School of Arts was officially opened in 1907 by Captain Philip Charley.

Higher altitudes such as the Blue Mountains and Kurrajong were considered beneficial for good health. Mary Wholohan operated Greendale, one of the first guesthouses. The *Sydney Morning Herald* of 1936 described it as being 'Homely, beautiful surroundings, all home cooked food, milk, cream' with tennis and horse riding.

The late Sid Sheldon, resident of Comleroy Road for many years, liked to reminisce of days gone by in his *Memories of Kurrajong*:

> And the orchards on the hillside
> And out on Comleroy
> The loads of fruit we used to pull,
> When I was quite a boy.

> But the orchards have vanished
> They are grazing pastures now.
> The only mark that still remains
> Are the furrows of the plough.

The Slopes is a locality situated along Comleroy Road, north east of Kurmond. Descendants of the McMahon family lived on The Slopes early this century. Mrs T. McMahon offered guesthouse accommodation at Mountain View Farm in the 1930s.

Cornwallis

Cornwallis is located on the lowlands of the fertile Hawkesbury River banks between Windsor and Richmond.

Shipowner Captain Michael Hogan arrived as master of the *Marquis of Cornwallis* carrying convicts to Sydney in 1796. He had vague connections to Lord Charles Cornwallis (1738-1805) 1st Marquis of Cornwallis who provided him with various opportunities. The ill-famed voyage is distinguished for its mutiny to seize the boat and sail to South America. During his three month stay in Sydney, he purchased Woodhay farm on the Hawkesbury River lowlands which he renamed Cornwallis Estate or Farm. Hogan appointed a manager to work the farm and went on to accumulate a fortune from his merchant and shipping activities, which included slave trading. He settled in New York and was involved in politics. Dying intestate, it took many years to settle his affairs. In 1861 the Hogan family sold the property.

In 1797, Governor John Hunter granted the first woman in the Hawkesbury, Jane Ezzy, 30 acres of land at Cornwallis. Jane was the 'free' wife of convict William Ezzy, who arrived in Australia in 1792.

Sketch of 1860 flood at Cornwallis by Rev Charles Garnsey. (Deborah Foster)

Cornwallis was the scene of a daring escape in 1803 when four convicts decided to make a bid for freedom by travelling over the Blue Mountains 'to China'. After 17 days they found nothing and, full of despair, decided to return. John Place, the only survivor, was found in a weakened state by a kangaroo hunter and some Aborigines and taken back to the Hawkesbury.

A horrific plane crash occurred in Cornwallis in 1929. Farmer Albert Smith was weeding on his farm when a RAAF aeroplane crashed, striking the farmer and decapitating him. Pilot and mechanic were pulled from the burning plane. Somerville the pilot was a friend of the Smiths and waved as the plane flew over the farm. Smith was a Richmond Council alderman. Later that year Somerville married Smith's daughter but tragedy struck when he was killed in a plane accident at Point Cook in 1936. In 1959 a Lockheed Neptune A89 on a routine training exercise from the RAAF Base experienced some mechanical problems and caught on fire. The plane crashed into Bakers Lagoon near Cornwallis Lane killing the eight crew members.

The lowlands at Cornwallis are fertile floodplains. Farmers have reaped the benefits and endured numerous floods. One flood in 1806 killed seven people. Thomas Leeson's barn, two houses, two horses, 70 pigs, 250 bushels of barley and wheat vanished into the swirling river. Leeson, with four family members and several others, was swept into the floodwaters clutching a barley mow. Astoundingly they endured the churning waters for seven miles, in the dark, on their flimsy life raft before reaching Wilberforce and being rescued by Richard Wallis who transferred them to the safety of his boat.

During the 1860 flood the river rose 11.21 metres at Windsor and swept away the Cornwallis Bridge. In 1867 unprepared farmers and their families had little choice but to climb on rooftops to escape the sudden raging waters which rose to 19.26 metres. Most were rescued but some were not so fortunate.

One very sad incident was the drowning of members of the Eather family at Cornwallis. The two Eather brothers, William, wife Catherine and their five children plus Thomas and his wife Emma and their six children spent nearly 20 hours clinging to a roof. Eventually William and Thomas and one of the boys were swept away and later rescued. Alas, sisters-in-law Catherine and Emma Eather and ten of their children drowned. William reported later, 'I heard the screams of my wife and children but could not see them; I fastened myself to the tree, and in a short time was rescued by a boat'. The recovered bodies were buried at Windsor Catholic Cemetery.

The Eather family in dire straits in the 1867 flood.
(Illustrated Sydney News 16 July 1867)

East Kurrajong

East Kurrajong follows the Bull Ridge from the intersection with Comleroy Road across to near Sackville. Some of the early pioneers of this district were the Buttsworth, Case and Packer families. When numerous small farming properties were made available by Conditional Purchase during the 1890s, the community expanded in an easterly direction. Chief crops included passionfruit, vegetables, citrus and stone fruit orchards. George Case developed a local variety of apricot called Glengarry.

In 1876 Reverend Monaghan, the Wesleyan minister at Windsor, requested a Provisional School be established at Buttsworth Swamp on Howes Creek, near East Kurrajong. Miss Jane Taylor was the first teacher. In 1891 a new school opened as Bull Ridge Provisional School. From 1922 the area became known as East Kurrajong.

Sports days and tea meetings were popular in small communities for raising money to build local halls. It was reported that a gathering assembled at Stanley Park in 1913, for a tea meeting. A number of races were held including a bicycle race, flag race and needle race. Apparently one woman cheated by having the needle already threaded yet still failed to win the contest. Tests of strength were also included such as wood chopping and the nail driving contest for women. After the tea meeting, about 20 couples continued the festivities by engaging in music and dancing into the early hours of the next morning.

RIGHT:
Ebenezer in the 1870s with the church sitting on the hill.
(GPO ML SLNSW)

Ebenezer – Portland Head

Portland Head is bounded by Portland Reach, Lower Crescent Reach, Upper Crescent Reach and Swallow Rock Reach. Portland Head Rock was named in 1805 after the rock formation, said to resemble the Duke of Portland. In 1802 Scottish and English free settlers arrived on the *Coromandel* and settled on grants of land along the Hawkesbury River in the area known as Portland Head. These settlers included John Turnbull, James Mein, John Johnstone, Andrew Johnston, James Davison, John Howe, George Hall and William Stubbs, plus their families. Other families with religious ties were Paul Bushell, John Grono, Thomas Arndell, Owen Cavanough, William Jacklin, John Suddis and Lewis Jones.

The first services were reputedly held under the gum tree opposite the present day Ebenezer Church. Owen Cavanough, a seaman who arrived in 1788, donated the land. A 'Society for promoting Christian values and the educating of youth' was formed in 1808 and construction of the church commenced the same year. Designed by Andrew Johnston, it was built on a ridge looking out over the Hawkesbury River and was in use by 1809. The stone entrance porch was added in 1929 and the vestry commenced in

1959. It is the oldest church in Australia and still in use today, with some of the congregation descendants of the original *Coromandel* settlers. The name Ebenezer Church was taken from the biblical reference in Samuel (7:12). Portland Head and the area west of the river has subsequently become known as Ebenezer. During the late 1980s extensive renovations of the church and Schoolmaster's House (circa 1817) were carried out.

Land adjoining the church was set aside as a burial ground and has many generations of the settlers interred there. Funeral processions often took place on the river. One of the last funerals arriving by river was John Grono in 1917. The first funeral to arrive by motor hearse was J. B. Johnston, real estate agent of McGraths Hill who died in 1925. The church was designed so that half

of the building could be used as a school. The school was established in 1810 with John Youl as teacher. The school was known as Portland Head Presbyterian Denominational School. Between 1874 and 1886 it operated as a provisional school known as Portland Head. As the population increased a purpose built school was established in Coromandel Road, opening as Ebenezer Public School in 1887. When this building was destroyed by bushfire in 1901, the school moved to its present day position. The school was sometimes used for community activities as there was no hall at Ebenezer.

Stannix Park is a two-storey stone house built by William Hall in 1839 and lovingly restored by the Hatherleys in the 1980s. The controversial Labour politician, and Premier of NSW, Jack Lang

(1876-1975) owned Myrtle Farm at Ebenezer and visited on the weekends. He named his bull Ebenezer. The cottage Ebenezer Villa, the original Turnbull house now known as Port Erringhi, built in the 1820s by John Turnbull, and the Johnston property held by the family until the 1950s and now called Portland Head Farm are all properties of local significance.

Port Erringhi was the name chosen by John Ellis when he established a ski park near Upper Crescent Reach, in the 1950s. It was named after *Erringhi* one of the Hawkesbury's riverboats that operated between 1912 and 1930s. It was earlier known as Bennetts Wharf. A ferry service operated between Pitt Town and Ebenezer from the 1820s and was taken over by the government in 1832 and operated until 1920.

OPPOSITE PAGE:
Stannix Park, Ebenezer prior to restoration.
(HCCLS)

LEFT:
Photo of an Ebenezer farm (looks like surname Brown on the fruit box), the piece of machinery next to the man sorting fruit is a horse powered whim. The horse would walk around in a circle turning the cogs of the large wheel and providing power to operate various pieces of farm equipment i.e. one horse power.
(HCCLS)

Freemans Reach

Freemans Reach is situated about 7 kilometres from Windsor and its fertile land is highly sought after. Some of the early Hawkesbury pioneers who settled at Freemans Reach include members of the Baldwin, Reynolds, Smith, Rutter, Nicholls, Robinson and Greentree families. The origin of the name is uncertain.

One of the earliest buildings in Freemans Reach is Reibycroft, the farmhouse said to be built by the ex-convict Mary Reibey in the 1820s. Mary apparently had the house built for her daughter, on land originally granted to her husband Thomas Reibey in 1803. Mary Reibey arrived in Australia as a convict in 1792 and when Thomas died in 1811 she was left to conduct their successful business. Enterprising Mary features on the $20 note.

There was a Congregational Church built at Freemans Reach in the late 1800s and demolished in 1918. Alexander Smith Jnr donated land known as Rainbow Hill now Kurmond Road, to the community in 1926. St Mark's Anglican Church was established on this site and services commenced in 1936.

Freemans Reach has always been a small village with a school, church, post office and general store. The community pitched in and built the Freemans Reach School of Arts in 1901. They made their own entertainment and dances and euchre parties were popular amusements. Old time dances still take place once a month in the School of Arts. Cricket and tennis were popular. First-class players such as Charlie Nicholls 1900–1983 and more recently, members of the Earle family were born in Freemans Reach.

By the 1850s, a day school was recorded and a public school was established at Freemans Reach

LEFT:
Perc Hutchison and Ron Jeffery at work on the farm at
Freemans Reach, 1900s.
(HCCLS)

OPPOSITE PAGE:
Aerial view of Freemans Reach, 1977. (RAAF)

BELOW:
Wilberforce Public School in the 1930s. Teacher Thomas
Fleming Campbell taught at Freemans Reach Public School
until 1931 and then at Wilberforce.
(Lorna Campbell)

was set up at the Freemans Reach School where schoolteacher Richard Todd operated it. The telephone service was connected in 1910. One memorable name connected to the postal service was Vida Greentree, or Aunty Vida who was Post Mistress from 1931 until 1965. Sir John Northcott, the Governor of NSW in 1960, unveiled the Freemans Reach monument, commemorating a Roll of Honour for both World Wars. Names on the monument include Hibbert, Kingham and Smith who lost their lives in World War I.

Land use has altered over the years. Farming turned to orchards and dairying. Turf farms have replaced the orchards. Along the lowlands on Freemans Reach Road are some

in 1867 and operated until 1872, re-opening in 1877. Thomas Fleming Campbell was the schoolteacher at Freemans Reach Public School between 1919 and 1927. He travelled each day by horse and sulky from Windsor.

The first official post office opened in 1884 and wonderful barns and farm buildings, reminiscent of the Hawkesbury's past. There are still farms in Freemans Reach growing vegetables and turf.

Glossodia

Glossodia was originally known as Currency Creek, named after the local creek. 'Currency' was the term used to describe native born as opposed to 'Sterling', those born in England. Currency Creek Public School was opened in 1898. The Postal Department established a receiving office in 1922 but as there was another Currency Creek in the country the name had to be changed. A public meeting was called in 1922 and Glossodia was the community's choice. Apparently a student took a small blue flower that grew around the creek bank to school. It was identified as 'glossodia' a dainty blue orchid. Mr Southwell, the teacher, suggested the new place name. On Boxing Day 1922 the name of the locality was changed at an official ceremony followed by a sports day which included athletic races, guessing competitions and a pillow fight. The school was renamed Glossodia Public School in 1923.

Glossodia Park Reserve is a remnant of Cumberland Plain woodland owned by Hawkesbury City Council. In recent years local Bushcare Volunteers have worked to regenerate and preserve it.

ABOVE:
Jack Lillis delivering the mail to Mavis Hutchison. (HCCLS)

LEFT:
Glossodia Public School class in 1954.
(Arthur Cooper)

Grose

The Grose River was named by Captain Paterson while exploring the Blue Mountains in 1793. The party were trying to reach the foothills but were obstructed by tree stumps and torrents. They did manage to proceed about 10 miles up the river and named it the Grose after Lieutenant-Governor Francis Grose. The other localities in this vicinity, such as Grose Valley, Grose Wold and Grose Vale take their name from the river. The Grose River rises near Mount Victoria and flows into the Nepean near Richmond and is about 56 kilometres in length. The Grose Valley is renowned for its spectacular gorges and scenery.

Francis Grose (1754-1814) was appointed as Lieutenant-Governor of the colony in 1789 to take command of the NSW Corps. He arrived in Sydney in early 1792 and when Phillip left later that year, Grose was left in command of the settlement. Essentially a military man, he made generous land grants to fellow military officers during his two year period in office. He is remembered for organising the first settlement in the Hawkesbury district.

During the 1850s various routes were considered for the proposed railway between Sydney and Bathurst. Several options were under consideration including the Grose. Between 1858 and 1859 a track was constructed in the Grose Valley by the Royal Engineers to complete survey

ABOVE:
Catch of the day. (HCCLS)

RIGHT:
Detail of Grose River Survey camp. (HCCLS)

Photographer Woodhill captures a group relaxing at the Grose River in the 1880s. (HCCLS)

View of the Grose Valley, late 19th century. Over 100 years later, little has changed. (HCCLS)

Hawkesbury River

The Hawkesbury-Nepean River is a 470 km system that begins near Goulburn, flows into the Warragamba Dam and continues into the Nepean, becoming the Hawkesbury River. The Colo and Macdonald Rivers flow into it further east before the mighty Hawkesbury meets the Pacific Ocean at Broken Bay. The Warragamba was dammed in 1961 to provide Sydney with water. The impact of settlement on the Hawkesbury

work which was difficult. The sharp bends in the river, deep gullies, sheer cliffs, landslides and floods lead to the abandonment of the project.

Water for Sydney was a great concern in the 1860s. Solutions included damming the Grose River. Alternatives were chosen but much of the Crown Land in the Grose was made a reserve, protecting it from development. In the 1890s a hydroelectric scheme was proposed but never got off the ground.

There was little land use in the Grose Valley. In the early 19th century Ben Carver leased land used mainly for cattle grazing. There was little clearing, and minimal construction of yards and huts. Carver's grant was acquired by members of the well-known Hordern family as the result of a debt.

The Grose River and valley have been a destination for bushwalkers and environmentalists since the 1800s. Most of the area is rugged and difficult to access but the efforts are rewarding. It

was very popular with early bushwalking clubs and women were able to wear men's clothing such as shorts in this secluded valley.

Grose Vale is a locality similar to many in the Hawkesbury district, without a central village. It is situated approximately 8 kilometres from Richmond and was originally known as Kurrajong South until 1929. A school was established here in 1871. Local resident Richard Skuthorpe lived in this area and called his property Grose Vale. It became the name of the locale. Grose Vale was also known as Little Kurrajong.

A school was established at Grose Wold in 1902 on land donated by Philip Charley of Belmont Park. The school building was moved from Kurrajong South Public School and renovated at the new site. The schools at Grose Wold and Grose Valley combined in 1977 to form Grose View Public School.

'The Hawkesbury Waltz' sheet music celebrates this famous waterway. (HCCLS)

*SS **Surprise** on the Hawkesbury River 1930s carrying a load of watermelons. (HCCLS)*

River and the surrounding environment has been considerable.

By 1789 Europeans toured the Hawkesbury River. Governor Phillip reported of the trip that he had named the river Hawkesbury, '... after the Lord Hawkesbury ... The great advantages of so noble a river, when a settlement can be made on its banks, will be obvious to your Lordship'.

Charles Jenkinson (1727-1808) was Lord Hawkesbury 1786 to 1796. At the time Phillip was exploring, he was President of the Council of Trade and Plantations. Created Baron Hawkesbury, of Gloucester in 1786 then Baron Hawkesbury from 1796, he contributed to the establishment of various British colonies. His son Robert Banks Jenkinson (1770-1828) was England's Prime Minister 1812 to 1827. Extinct in 1851, the titles were revived in 1905.

The river was used as a transport route for over a century and was later crossed by punt or bridge. Andrew Thompson operated the first boatbuilding business and other boatbuilders included Daniel Smallwood, Charles Beasley and Jonathan Griffiths. John Grono was noted as one of the finest shipbuilders in the colony. Boatbuilding yards were established on the riverbanks and the majority of materials were obtained locally.

A group pose for photographer Woodhill while they boil the billy on the banks of the Hawkesbury River. (HCCLS)

ABOVE:
The Hawkesbury River in flood in the late 19th century.
(HCCLS)

OPPOSITE PAGE:
Richmond Bridge under water circa 1910.
(HCCLS)

LEFT:
A crowd gather at Thompson Square to look at the
floodwaters at Windsor in 1879.
(ML SLNSW)

The riverboat trade carrying fruit was an enormous industry. Hundreds of boats transported all sorts of produce from farms up and down the river to the Sydney markets or the Windsor railhead. Boats of up to 100 tons were navigated to the Windsor Wharf with about 10 large boats berthing a week. The river was silting up by the 1880s because of flooding, making it difficult for the larger boats to get to Windsor. The number of large boats berthing by this time had decreased by 90 per cent. A regular steam service was implemented as these boats did not require deep water. The Hawkesbury Steam Navigation Company was formed in the late 1880s. This company operated on a co-operative basis with the ships carrying passengers, cargo and delivering goods. Some of the well-known boats were the SS *Hawkesbury*, SS *Kallawatta*, SS *Erringhi* and later the SS *Surprise II*. The riverboats worked up until the 1940s when cheap road transport became too competitive.

Over the years, the beauty of the Hawkesbury River has entranced explorers and travellers. During the 1870s, the author Anthony Trollope (1815-1882) travelled along the Hawkesbury. He wrote in his publication *Australia and New Zealand in 1873* '… as we reached the bluffs and high banks of the lower reaches, the scene was changed, and as the afternoon wore itself away we steamed down among the river scenery as lovely as any which I ever beheld'. Trollope compares the Hawkesbury with the Rhine and Mississippi and writes, 'The Hawkesbury has neither castles nor islands, nor has it bright clear water like the Rhine. But the headlands are higher and the bluffs are bolder, and the turns and manoeuvres of the course which the waters have made for themselves are grander, and to me more enchanting, than those of either the European or American river.'

Landscape Arthur Streeton (1867-1943), one of the founders of the Heidelberg School, visited the Hawkesbury in the 1890s. He painted *The purple noon's transparent might* from The Terraces near North Richmond. The painting, an oil on canvas, is owned by the National Gallery of Victoria. Streeton painted several scenes of the district, as did Julian Ashton, Charles Conder and early Colonial artist Joseph Lycett. Some of these works are cited in 'Hawkesbury's Artist Trail'.

The Hawkesbury is notorious for its floods. Shortly after settlement, the Hawkesbury settlers experienced their first flood. Long periods of drought followed by unusually high rainfalls resulted in the Hawkesbury experiencing 27 major floods during the 19th century. Early settlers were unaware of flooding and settled themselves and their families on the fertile alluvial plains close to the riverbanks. Loss of human life, crops, livestock and housing was extremely high and eventually the settlers moved their homes to higher ground. With experience of floods and flood patterns and the development of technology, serious damage was reduced. The worst flood experienced in the Hawkesbury was the great flood of 1867. Following an enormous amount of rain the river rose rapidly, catching many residents unaware. The river was recorded at Windsor at 19.3 metres higher than normal. Large areas were inundated and there was considerable loss of life. Severe damage and hardship occurred. The height of floods ranges from a minor flood less than 7.6 metres above the normal river level at Windsor Bridge, to a major flood that is greater than 9.5

LEFT:
Swimming in the shoals of the Hawkesbury c1910.
(HCCLS)

metres. In the 20th century there were three significant floods recorded. The worst was in 1961 when the river rose 15.1metres. In 1964 it was recorded at 14.5 metres and in 1978, the river rose to 14.3 metres, the last major flood.

The Hawkesbury Regatta Club was formed in 1845 to foster aquatic sports. Races were held for two and four oared boats, sculls and canoes. Regattas were held regularly along the river and the Grono family were unbeaten participants. Sculling flourished with local sportsman Peter Kemp becoming the World Champion in the 1880s.

The length and breadth of the Hawkesbury River suits the popular sport of waterskiing and powerboat racing. The first waterskiing club to be formed in Australia in 1950 was at Sackville. Early identities in the sport included George Andronicus, Ray Leighton, Bill McLachlan and 'Gelignite Jack' Murray. The Bridge-to-Bridge race has been held regularly since 1934. From Wisemans Ferry to Windsor, high-speed, aerodynamic powerboats race up and down the river. Between Penrith and Wisemans Ferry there are between 20-25 ski-parks operating.

From the 1830s to 1850s, recreational excursions took place. Day trips and holidays were becoming more popular and as the Hawkesbury was accessible by river and later by train, it became a popular destination. Visitors often took the steamer from Sydney to Windsor via the Hawkesbury River and then caught the train home. Picnics on the Hawkesbury River suited motor tours.

RIGHT:
The Warragamba River was dammed in 1961 to supply Sydney with water, photographed on 2 August 1990. (RAAF)

Swimming became popular in the 1890s. In 1896, the Mile Championship of Australasia race was held at Windsor with contestants from interstate and New Zealand. With many drownings, clubs were formed to teach swimming and most swimming took place in the river. A meeting of enthusiastic women to form a Swimming Association in Windsor in 1896 was attended by about 30 ladies. Sadly swimming has not been encouraged in the Hawkesbury River since the late 1980s due to water quality.

Population pressure is taking its toll. Recently the Hawkesbury River became choked with salvinia weed. Harvesters have collected the weed but the cost to control it is overwhelming. The river needs nurturing and care to maintain water quality and health of the fauna if it is to have a future.

ABOVE:
Jennings family picnic on the banks of the Hawkesbury River at Windsor. (M Nichols)

OPPOSITE PAGE ABOVE:
Recreational swimming in the Hawkesbury River, near Windsor circa 1930s. (Lorna Campbell)

OPPOSITE PAGE BOTTOM LEFT:
Speedboats on the Hawkesbury in the 1970s. (HCCLS)

OPPOSITE PAGE BOTTOM RIGHT:
Marie McLachlan (1928-2003) was one of the pioneer water skiers on the Hawkesbury River in the 1950s. (Chris McLachlan)

RIGHT:
A riverboat rests in the willows on the Hawkesbury. (HCCLS)

Hobartville

William Cox Jnr acquired a total of 400 acres on the outskirts of Richmond between 1814 and 1818. By 1828 he had built Hobartville a grand Georgian two storey mansion. It was established as a working farm and continues the same landuse today. Elizabeth Cox wrote in a letter in 1828: '... all the furniture required for the carpenters is to come from England ...' and several months later, 'We are getting on rapidly with the new house. The carpenters are now finishing the cedar timber in the bedrooms.'

The estate passed to Sloper Cox, son of William Jnr and was purchased by Andrew Town (1840-1890) in 1877 who ran it as a successful horse breeding and cattle stud. Captain William Holborrow, Town's brother-in-law, was the live-in manager. Hobartville was renowned for its famous sires, and breeding thoroughbreds and draught horses, Andrew Town imported horses which improved Australian bloodstock. Town was a member of various racing clubs and a judge for the Australian Jockey Club and Sydney Turf Cub. Town also bred pigs and kept a dairy. In 1879 the famous sales commenced under the oak trees at

Hobartville. Special trains ran from Sydney to Richmond. The sales, attended by huge crowds, were extremely successful and good food and drink were served in a marquee set up in the grounds. In the 1888 drought Town became bankrupt and suddenly died. Hobartville estate was repossessed by the mortgagees, Hon. William Alexander Long and George Hill. In 1900 the estate was purchased by Percy Reynolds and continued to be run by his son Raymond who established a famous Hereford stud that operated until 1958.

In the 1950s and 60s part of the estate was subdivided and sold forming the locality of Hobartville. A school, a park and several shops were established. Some of the streets were given names relating to the history of the Hobartville estate such as Cox, Town, Luttrell, Sloper, Onus and Holborrow, as well some named after Town's famous horses such as Grand Flanuer and Childe Harold. The equine industry remains an important business in the district and today the remainder of the original Hobartville estate is still used as a Horse Stud.

Catchpole Avenue in Hobartville reminds us of the convict Margaret Catchpole who was transported for stealing a horse. She arrived on the *Nile* in 1801 and worked for many years as a nursemaid for the Dight family. Her notorious life has created many local legends. A number of her letters have survived and provide a picture of the district in the early 1800s. She is buried without a marker in St Peter's Cemetery in Richmond.

LEFT:
The splendid Hobartville house.
(HCCLS)

Kurmond

Kurmond is a small village located along Bells Line of Road, between Kurrajong and North Richmond. It was originally known as Longleat after a property in the area. Most of the area now known as Kurmond was originally granted to David Horton Snr, a convict who arrived in 1791. Horton was granted the land in the 1820s and sold it to the Bootle's, adjoining property owners. It is not known who established Longleat Farm but there was a cottage constructed apparently in the 1860s that remained in the Bootle and Hoskisson's family until the early 1900s. In 1913 Ted Peck acquired the property and subdivided the area around Longleat Lane.

Following World War I, a soldier settlement scheme was established in the Kurrajong-Kurmond area. With special conditions attached, about 46 blocks of between 30 and 35 acres were allotted. The houses were basic two bedroom weatherboard cottages. Some of the families who settled in Kurmond as a result of the soldier settlement found it hard to make a living and ended up having to forfeit the properties as they had a poor knowledge of farming, the land was unproductive and it was during the 1930s depression. Some families sold fruit and vegetables on the roadside.

In 1929 Ernest and Rosa Merriman built Longview at Kurmond. Ten years later it was purchased by John and Ethel Navin and renamed Kamilaroi. It operated as a thriving guesthouse. The Navins also ran the adjacent General Store and sold petrol. Longleat Public School was established in 1920 and the school was renamed Kurmond Public School in 1926. The name Kurmond is apparently a blend of 'KURrajong' and 'RichMOND'.

Descendants of the convict David Dunston of Wilberforce included four brothers who owned land between Grose Vale and Kurrajong Heights. They built some magnificent homes including Cooraba (1894), Westbury, Warranave and Inverary. The nearby street, Inverary Drive, is named for the property and is possibly the original entrance to the house.

RIGHT:
View of Kurmond from Longview which was built in 1929 by the Merriman's and later became the Kamilaroi Guesthouse. (HCCLS)

FROM "LONGVIEW", KURMOND.

Kurrajong

Located at the base of the Blue Mountains, Kurrajong, Kurrajong Heights and Kurrajong Hills are in the region called Kurrajong. The population in this area has almost doubled in the last 20 years.

Earlier variations of Kurrajong include Kurry Jung and Curryjong. Kurrajong is reportedly the Aboriginal name for the *Brachychiton populneus*, a fodder and shade tree. A number of earlier explorers investigated the area including Lieutenant Dawes and George Caley who visited the area in 1804. Governor Lachlan Macquarie toured the district in 1810 and noted in his journal , 'We rode through fine open forest and hilly country for about five miles to the foot of Curry Jung Hill, which is very long and steep to ascend … and from whence we a had a very grand noble prospect of the low Green Hills.' Explorers Benjamin Singleton and William Parr departed from Wheeny Creek in the early 1800s searching for a route north. Singleton had established a water mill on the banks of Wheeny Creek and Samuel Leverton, and later John Town, operated mills in the area. Two millstones from this period were moved to Memorial Park in Kurrajong village.

Cut Rock, the pass near Kurrajong Heights was the deviation along the Bells Line of Road, and the name is still in use today. At Cut Rock the Kurrajong Fault is visited by students studying geology and is listed on the Register of the National Estate. A property at Kurrajong Heights called Tabaraga gave its name to an area of Bells Line to Bilpin. There was also Tabaraga Ridge. Netley Hill is now the Kurrajong Hills area. Kurrajong Heights was originally known as The Big Hill or Douglass' Hill after a local family.

Kurrajong Railway Station in 1926. (SRA SRNSW)

View of Wheeny Creek. (HCCLS)

NETLEY HILL, KURRAJONG.

LEFT:
On the ascent of
Netley Hill in the
1940s.
(HCCLS)

KURRAJONG FROM NETLEY HILL.

LEFT:
Orchards at
Kurrajong as seen
from Netley Hill.
(HCCLS)

In 1823 Archibald Bell Jnr established his route from Richmond via Kurrajong to the Coxs River and it was named Bells Line of Road. Robert Hoddle, the assistant-surveyor, inspected and marked the new route with Bell but it was to be many years before the road was built. Sarah Mathew, wife of the surveyor Felton Mathew, recorded in her 1834 journal that Bell was shown this route by an Aboriginal woman. The Mathews were known to the Bells.

The Bells Line of Road was used by drovers and travellers and inevitably inns sprang up in convenient stopping places. Resting yards were often provided for stock and food and accommodation were available. Donnybrook near Wheeny Creek and the Currency Lass were two early inns. Goldfinders Rest was operated by John Lamrock from 1851 until 1868 and then taken over by his son-in-law John Benson. The inn became the Wheeny Creek branch of the post office in 1860 and was renamed the Kurrajong Post Office in 1868. It continued until 1916 when a new post office was built. Ivy Lodge was available for accommodation in Kurrajong in the late 1820s. It is now known as Lochiel and operates as a restaurant. In the 1860s the Mrs Powell, Sherwood and Douglass kept outstanding establishments. In later years, Miss Stewart provided accommodation for tourists and visitors at Glencuffe at Kurrajong.

The main village of Kurrajong was located through the Wheeny (which was then the main part of the village of Kurrajong). John Lamrock lived in a house further up the ridge which was called Plynlimmon and also bought another property in the area called Woodburne. He donated part of the land adjacent to Plynlimmon for the site of the Anglican church. The Kurrajong Heights Hotel was established in the late 1920s by

Mr H. Peck and was considered very modern. It burned down in 1974 and later was rebuilt.

Kurrajong and its surrounds have been visited or lived in by some recognizable names. Some of the pioneering families include Hurst, Shepherd and Wilson. The Hon James Comrie MLC and his wife Sophia lived in Northfield built by Samuel North at Kurrajong Heights in 1857. Comrie gave to various charities and local appeals, assisted those in need and helped locals promote their communities. Louisa Atkinson (1834-1872) was Australia's first native-born novelist, a keen botanist and artist. In 1859 she moved to Kurrajong Heights and lived with her invalid mother on the property Fernhurst. Atkinson's articles and natural art sketches were sometimes published in the Sydney newspapers. On her frequent jaunts from Fernhurst she discovered botanical species which bear her name. Louisa was friends with Rev William Woolls and he sometimes accompanied her on her expeditions, as did Mrs Selkirk, wife of the Richmond doctor. They are recorded as defiantly wearing men's attire whilst on their outings. She married James Calvert and moved back to Berrima but died in 1872 soon after giving birth to a daughter. In 1979 a memorial was unveiled in Powell Park in memory of this botanist by the Kurrajong Heights Garden Club.

By the 1870s Kurrajong district had three schools. There was a private school conducted at Kurrajong Heights plus two denominational schools. Mrs Barton operated a ladies seminary in the 1860s. A Catholic school operated on the corner of Bells Line of Road and Comleroy Road, as well as an Anglican school. In 1878 the Anglican became Kurrajong North Public School. A new building opened in 1882. In 1890 the school was extended and in 1896 a second teacher

was appointed due to high enrolments. Rev H. Plume was the minister at St Stephen's Anglican from 1888 to 1891. To supplement his income he started to take a number of students and prepare them to matriculation level in 1890. The following year he acquired Stokesleigh at Kurrajong Heights and opened a grammar school naming it Barker College after the Bishop. Plume had earlier worked at St Paul's College at the University of Sydney. In 1896 Plume transferred the school to Hornsby. Kurrajong Public School opened in 1929.

St Gregory's Catholic Church was consecrated at Kurrajong in 1840. It was used as both church and schoolhouse. It was replaced with the present building, opened in 1904. The *Australian Churchman* newspaper stated 'A more beautiful spot could not be found in the diocese; in fact, from it's elevated position this sacred edifice when completed will form quite a conspicuous landmark.' St Stephen the Martyr was completed in 1869. St James Anglican at Kurrajong Heights was built in 1889.

St David's was established at Kurrajong Heights in 1886 by the Presbyterians. A small cemetery is located adjacent with many local families buried there. Early graves are those of Joseph Douglass who died in 1865 and his wife Mary Orr Burgess who died in 1857. Joseph Douglass was a convict who arrived in 1815. His wife Mary followed her husband from Ireland eight years later, and they settled at Ivy Lodge at Kurrajong Heights in the late 1820s. Their hospitality was noted in the newspapers of the time and by Sarah Mathew and Lady Jane Franklin, wife of the Tasmanian Governor.

With suitable soil, altitude and climate, the Kurrajong area was well suited for citrus growing as well as apples, passionfruit, bananas, custard apples and grapes. In the 19th and early 20th century peas, tomatoes, beans, rockmelons and watermelons were cultivated and Kurrajong was known as the 'kitchen garden of Sydney.' In the 1890s the citrus business was in its peak with some orchardists exporting their goods. Kurrajong provided firewood and tons of wattlebark, used in the tanning industry. It was sometimes called 'Kurrajong wool' and assisted many families during the depression years.

During the 1880s the community proposed that the railway line be extended from Richmond to Kurrajong and it opened in 1926. There were several stations on the line including the unattended station at North Richmond and sidings for passengers to catch the train. The main engine that ran on this line was known as The Pansy. Running at a loss and following flood damage and landslides, the line was officially closed in 1952. The voluntary group known as TRAK was recently formed and hopes to re-establish part of the line and run a tourist train.

Kurrajong was promoted to tourists in the 1920s as 'The Once Neglected Paradise'. To find bellbirds, the gardens, good accommodation for those 'desiring a restful holiday', the Kurrajong district was seen as just the place. The 'health resort Kurrajong cannot be surpassed with its fine bracing climate and views second to none in the state'. There were several guesthouses and lodges including Belmore Lodge run by Miss Jennings, Stokesleigh run by Mr Withers and Mountain View run by Mary Peck. Tennis, shooting, swimming, fishing and nature study were available for the visitor. In the early 1920s, every Saturday night a movie was shown at Hart's Hall at Kurrajong, followed by a dance.

Laughtondale

Laughtondale is downstream from Wisemans Ferry. It is named after John Laughton who came from Scotland to Sydney in 1836. He was employed as a carpenter on the *Stirling Castle* but jumped ship on arrival. The boat departed Sydney travelling north only to be shipwrecked near Gladstone. One of the several survivors, Eliza Fraser, was enslaved by the Aborigines before being rescued.

John Laughton was a Methodist lay preacher who took up land on the Hawkesbury River which became known as Laughtondale. With his background as a ship's carpenter Laughton became a boatbuilder and, with his family and the Greentrees, built boats on the Lower Hawkesbury. One of their well-known vessels was the wooden steamship the *Kallawatta* built in 1906 and operated until 1920 when it was taken over by the Hawkesbury Steamship Company. The *Kallawatta* was used to transport fruit from the orchards along the Lower Hawkesbury to the Sydney markets.

Lady Hawkesbury *tourist boat at Laughtondale in 1987. (HCCLS)*

Leets Vale

Matthew Everingham the younger was granted land in about 1816 and his farm was known as Berry Hill as was the locality. It later changed to Bluetts Bight. Early pioneers include members of the Everingham, Herps, Chaseling and Leet families.

Jonathan Leet arrived in the colony in 1857 as an assisted immigrant. He arrived with his brother and met up with their uncle, Israel Leet who was living at Webbs Creek. Jonathan was married in 1862 to Catherine Rose, settling for a period at Webbs Creek. He purchased a vessel which he used to take produce to Windsor. After the 1867 flood he sold his boat and purchased property at Bluetts Bight above Wisemans Ferry. Leet renamed the property Leets Vale several years later. He saw the fruit industry as viable and established a nursery and an orchard. He joined the Wesleyan Methodists, a very popular religion in the Lower Hawkesbury, and was a local preacher for 47 years. He passed away in 1921 aged 92 years.

Religious services were held in homes, barns or out in the open prior to a church being constructed. Services gave worshippers the chance to interact socially. Church services were originally held at Leets Vale in the home of the Woodburys and later the Chaselings. Jonathan Leet donated land for the first Methodist Church at Leets Vale (1876) a simple slab building with a shingle roof, replaced by a second church in 1937. Chaseling family cemetery is also located at Leets Vale.

Leets Vale covers both sides of the Hawkesbury River. The school was located on the Webbs Creek side whilst the post office and church were on the Wisemans Ferry side. This often meant rowing a boat across the river to attend school or post a letter or vice versa.

A post office opened in 1887. Israel (Tom) Leet Snr was the first postmaster followed by his son, Jonathan who carried the mail from 1921 until 1934, on horseback and then by Harley Davidson motor bike. The mailman also delivered the newspapers, groceries and medicines. The mail came from Brooklyn via the river to Wisemans Ferry and was then picked up by the postal workers.

Barney Morley, Reg Green and Desmond Morley loading melons at Chaseling's Wharf at Leets Vale. (HCCLS)

Londonderry

Londonderry is a small village located about 4 kilometres southwest of Richmond. Thomas Kendall was granted 30 acres of land in 1831 and named it Londonderry. Nutt Road is named after Robert Nutt who was the Mayor of Castlereagh from 1946 until 1947. He resided in Londonderry and operated the local store and post office.

Edith Marney (nee Martin) lived most of her life in Londonderry and recorded her memories shortly after she turned 100 in 1996. Moving to Londonderry with her family in 1903, she remembered there was very little there, except bush. Her father started a dairy which was unsuccessful. With her two brothers she walked into Richmond to attend school. A tramcar was set up opposite the school in 1935 for Sunday School and monthly church services. Edith's father donated land for a hall in Londonderry and it was named the Robert Martin Hall.

A trotting and racing club was established on the outskirts of Richmond, at Londonderry, in 1912. From 1969 it has operated as Richmond Racecourse and is a popular trotting track. Kurrajong Trotting Club was formed in 1906. This club often held picnic races near Redbank Creek at North Richmond. Prior to this the Hawkesbury Show had specific sections and in 1890 a special class for trotting was introduced.

Andrew Town was instrumental in the introduction of trotting to Australia. Town imported Childe Harold in 1882 from America for £3935. Harold Park is named in honour of Childe Harold. As well as Town, there were several other Hawkesbury residents involved with breeding trotters. They included Dr G. Slate, a dentist from America who leased Fairfield House from the McQuade family and established a training track. Slade imported the stallion Huon from America which cost £2000. C. J. Roberts operated a successful trotting stud at Prestonville at Windsor. Trotting was very popular in Riverstone and the Moulds, Woods, Dawson and Phillis families were some who were involved.

Trotting was a popular sport in the late 19th century in the Hawkesbury district. (HCCLS)

Lower Portland

Lower Portland is the area north and downstream of Sackville and south and upstream of Leets Vale, where the Colo flows into the Hawkesbury River. Several fine buildings remain in the Lower Portland area. Dargle was built in 1831, by Andrew Doyle, an Irish ex-convict who arrived in 1803, for his son John Frederick. The date of the building '1831' and the initials 'J. F. D.' are carved in the stone above the entrance. This is now one of the biggest ski-parks located along the Hawkesbury River.

Another pleasant home still standing is the property called Venetiaville. The Kemp family originally built this in the 1860s but it was

The Lower Portland ferry in the 1930s. (HCCLS)

partially destroyed by fire in 1908 and then rebuilt in the 1920s. Peter Kemp was born in 1853, near the mouth of the Colo River and taught himself to row on both the Colo and Hawkesbury Rivers. Sculling at the time was very popular in Australia. He started racing in the 1880s and eventually went to England to train in 1886 returning the following year. In 1888 Kemp became the World Sculling Champion. At his peak, Kemp was hailed as a brilliant oarsman.

The earliest headstone at Lower Portland is John Pendergast who died in 1830. Other headstones are for Nash, Whalen, Reilly, Lamb and Reed, mainly in the 1840s. (Michelle Nichols)

In 1867 a provisional school was established and became Lower Portland Public School in 1869. The school was located at the junction of the Hawkesbury and Colo Rivers and some of the students had to be rowed across the river in a boat. The first known teacher was Walter King, who later finished his career at Ebenezer. A stone school replaced a timber structure in 1874. The student numbers fluctuated over the years and it closed in 1996.

The 1867 flood destroyed many of the churches lower down the river. St John's Anglican and the Methodist Chapel, both at Lower Portland, were destroyed. Originally Methodist, now Uniting, the foundation stone for the current endearing little Church at Lower Portland was laid in 1884. The land was donated by the Loder family and the church faces the river. A parsonage was opened in 1839.

A Georgian stone farmhouse known as Peacock's is located along River Road. It was built in 1826 by native born John Jenkins Peacock and a second storey was added in 1830. In 1831 the Peacock family endured a home invasion by runaway convicts. *The Australian* newspaper reported the intruders, 'proceeded with the utmost deliberation to collect all the moveables they could find of any value, with some cash, and having asked and partaken of refreshment, wished Peacock and his wife good night.' Peacock organised a posse and tracked down the thieves. The district constable shot one of the convicts in the arm in the ensuing scuffle and he had to have his arm amputated at a later date. Peacock had his stolen goods returned.

John Pendergast, a convict arriving on the *Minerva* in 1800 acquired land on the Hawkesbury River by 1808 and it became known as Half Moon Farm. His son James inherited the property in the early 1830s and provided land for a Catholic School to be built in 1838. There is no record that the school was constructed but perhaps it was the chapel known as St Rose of Lima that was built near the Upper Branch of the Hawkesbury and doubled as a schoolhouse. St Rose of Lima was opened on St Rose's Feast Day in 1840 and operated for the next 25 years. The church washed away in the 1867 flood. This property is now run by Hawkesbury City Council as a reserve. There is also a small historical cemetery located on Half Moon Farm.

Macdonald

Macdonald encompasses the area of the Macdonald River and valley as well as St Albans. It was explored by Governor Phillip's party in 1789. They travelled up the tributary and camped. Phillip named it the First Branch. The First Branch, also called the Lower Branch, was renamed the Macdonald River after John Macdonald. He was an ex-convict who arrived in 1812 and who used the valley to transport stock to Wollombi and the Hunter Valley.

The main link between Macdonald and the outer world was by the river. From the time of settlement until about the 1880s boats plied up and down the river as far as St Albans carrying produce and passengers to both Sydney and Windsor. Frequent flooding increased the silt so that it became quite shallow and unnavigable. Other routes included the Great North Road built by convict labour, the road through Shepherds Gully and the alternative route north to Wollombi and the Hunter Valley. The river could be crossed at what was originally known as Butlers Ford, later a punt operated here called Books Ferry. During the early 19th century the inhabitants of the Macdonald wrote to the Governor requesting land be set aside as a common and it was made official in 1853. It is one of the few commons still in use today. This road through the common can still be accessed today and is a picturesque excursion. The St

Early Macdonald River Crossing. (HCCLS)

A view of the village of St Albans. (WC ML SLNSW)

Albans Road and Settlers Road were constructed in the 1900s and the Macdonald was crossed at St Albans by a composite truss bridge that replaced an earlier bridge upstream damaged in the 1889 flood. The truss bridge was designed by De Burgh and officially opened in 1903. The bridge is classified as a significant Australian timber bridge.

The Macdonald Valley community built numerous churches throughout the valley. St Joseph's Catholic Church at Central Macdonald had land donated by John Watson to establish a Catholic Church and the foundation stone was laid by Bishop John Bede Polding in 1839. The church was to be the cathedral of the Hawkesbury but the population did not warrant it. Finished about 1845, there is a cemetery adjacent to it with burials dating from the 1840s. The church was used as a monastery during the 1850s but went into decline around 1880. Sadly the church was ravaged by bush fire in 1898 leaving only the stonework shell.

Roger Sheehy donated land for Our Lady of Loreto Catholic Church, opened by 1842. The church, now on private property, is in ruins. The cemetery adjacent predates the church with some of the headstones dating from the 1830s. Several public cemeteries are located within the Macdonald Valley, as well as numerous private ones, restricted to the public. The headstones record the names of many of the pioneering individuals and families that lived in this isolated yet peaceful valley. Noteworthy are the names of the Jurd, Fernance, Sternbeck, Walter and Morris families.

The influence of the Wesleyan Methodists was powerful throughout the Macdonald Valley. John Joseph Walker lived in the Macdonald from the 1830s and four of his sons became preachers, as did many of his descendants, including the Rev Dr Sir Alan Walker, the evangelist and founder of Lifeline, who died in 2003. The first Methodist meeting was held in 1838 and the circuit minister then visited the district regularly. Sometime in the 1830s Mrs Elizabeth Jurd donated land from her property to establish a chapel.

Travellers to St Albans resting. (WC ML SLNSW)

A small building was constructed and was commonly known as Jurd's Chapel. In the 1960s it was falling into disrepair but was saved by being resited at Vision Valley in Arcadia.

There are numerous reminders of the past in the Macdonald Valley. The Victoria Inn is a two storey sandstone building constructed in the early 1830s by David Cross. It was first opened in 1838 as the Queen Victoria Inn and later Sternbeck's Inn. Primrose Hill was established by emancipated convict Christian Sternbeck who arrived in 1802 on the *Perseus*. He purchased and was granted land in the Macdonald and constructed his home some time before the 1820s. It was remodelled by the 1840s and has recently had considerable renovations. William Bailey was a convict who arrived on the *Matilda* in 1791. He built the The Glen and was the patriarch of a large family that still lives on in the Valley today. He died in 1826 and was the first burial in the private cemetery on site.

Initially there were decisions to establish various town centres in the Macdonald during the 1820s. Benton, Macdonald, Howick and Bullock Wharf can be seen on early maps of the area. Eventually St Albans was gazetted as the official name in 1841, the name of the home town of settler William Bailey.

A Methodist Church was established in St Albans after land was granted in 1853. The current building was built in 1902 from the original material. The Anglicans in St Albans used a timber church and school house until 1863 when a stone church was constructed which was renovated and altered in 1896. 'Price Morris Cottage' is a slab cottage built by Price Morris between 1835 and 1837 and the first Methodist service was apparently held there in 1838. The house was derelict in the 1970s but has been recently been lovingly restored to its former glory.

There have been several hotels and inns operating in the Macdonald Valley but the Settlers Arms Inn is the only licensed hotel remaining. This attractive two storey stone building was built about 1848 by John Sullivan and originally called the Travellers Rest. The 1889 flood, which was the highest recorded flood in the Macdonald, rose to the second storey of this hotel. It is a popular tourist destination for Sydney weekenders. The Industrious Settler Inn was constructed in 1834 by free settler Aaron Walters north of St Albans and was licensed in 1837.

Originally a court house was located on the flats in the 1850s but this was damaged in the 1889 flood. A stone courthouse was built higher up the ridge on Upper Macdonald Road in the 1890s and local magistrates held sittings here until court matters were transferred to Windsor. There were several denominational and private schools situated in the valley. A government school operated in the Macdonald Valley from 1850.

Riverboat moored on the Macdonald River. (HCCLS)

McGraths Hill

The earliest land grants were given to Andrew Thompson and William Balmain. Thompson was granted 120 acres on the banks of South Creek and he built the residence known as West Hill Farm. This was commonly known as the Red House possibly because of the hue of the bricks. James McGrath, a convict who arrived in 1802, purchased 30 acres of land from the estate of Andrew Thompson in 1815. He built the first road between Parramatta and Windsor in 1813 and the Windsor Wharf in 1814 with John Howe. McGrath died in 1833, the locality taking on the name of McGraths Hill.

Charles Sommers a free settler who arrived in 1816 was employed as a clerk, innkeeper and headmaster. Sommers purchased the Red Brick Farm in 1832 for £450 and during the 1840s farmed the property. In the late 1840s times were difficult as he had to provide for a family of 12. Around 1848 he subdivided the farm named The Village of Sommers Town and the lots were

ABOVE:
The Australian Hotel at McGraths Hill at the turn of the century. (HCCLS)

OPPOSITE PAGE:
View of Windsor upon the River Hawkesbury NSW from McGraths Hill painted by Joseph Lycett. (NLA)

LEFT:
One of the splendid old barns that once dotted the Hawkesbury landscape, taken at McGraths Hill in 1979. (HCCLS)

auctioned off. In 1850 the Wesleyan community of Windsor purchased land at Sommers Town (now McGraths Hill) to establish a burial ground. Previously the Wesleyans were buried in the Presbyterian cemetery on land now adjacent to the Windsor Railway Station. In 1851 the first internment occurred, that of Rebecca Cavanough who died aged six days. The plot was purchased at a cost of £1.

Horse races were conducted at the racetrack known as Killarney which possibly took its name from Killarney Chain of Ponds nearby. In 1833 attendees reported a great race day which included a military band and wonderful entertainment. James 'Toby' Ryan recalled in *Reminiscences of Australia* that 'Every kind of amusement imaginable was going on, nine pins, puppet shows, the devil among the tailors, with lollypop and cake stalls … skittles and gambling of

every description, with an occasional fight through the day.'

In McGraths Hill little of the past has survived. Fortunately there are the cottages on the Windsor side of the hotel, the hotel and the cemetery. Spring Hill is located in Beddek Street, named after the Windsor lawyer who practised from 1828 to 1852. Spring Hill is a pleasing historic property with house, outbuildings and splendid slab barn. It once belonged to the Johnston family.

Two very large silos were constructed during the 19th century on the intersection of Windsor Road and Pitt Town Road. Fruit and vegetable stalls were a common sight near the silos but the silos were demolished in the late 1960s. The area was subdivided in the 1970s into residential lots.

Alternatively spelt as McGraths and Magrath Hill during the 19th century, the area is now known as McGraths Hill.

Maraylya

Maraylya was originally known as North Rocks and later as Forrester. In 1868 Rev Charles Garnsey, the Anglican minister in Windsor, proposed that a school be established in the area. Approval was given for a provisional school to operate and a simple weatherboard classroom was built that year.

In 1895 a post office was opened with the name Forrester, possibly after one of the Hawkesbury pioneering families living in the area. By 1920 the name was again changed to Maraylya the meaning of which is not known. It was noted in the *Windsor and Richmond Gazette* in 1920 that, 'The name of Forrester has been changed to Maraylya. The people will be some time getting accustomed to this outlandish name.'

It was a small community with most inhabitants operating small farms and orchards. Citrus, stone fruits, passionfruit and vegetables were grown. The Maraylya Hall was built in the 1920s and used for a variety of events. Entertainment was usually improvised and picnics were popular. Land was donated by David Whitmore for a church in the 1930s in what is now known as St Johns Road. Sid Kemp and David Whitmore built it and it opened in 1939. Most of the community purchased goods from grocers, drapers and butchers who called regularly, or visited Windsor. During the 1950s Fred Gallagher ran a small store next to the school in Neich Road. Neich Road is named after Alec Neich who was a noted saddler and harness maker. Boundary Road marks the boundary between the two local government areas of Windsor and Baulkham Hills.

Mountain Lagoon

This area was discovered in the early 1830s by surveyors. George Matcham Pitt conducted the sale of the subdivision of Mountain Lagoon in 1868. The first block paid for was John Stewart's 50 acre farm on which he was squatting. John Stewart died of a snake bite received on the property. His son Wilton and his wife later lived there and when he died, his wife and daughters Myra and Ivy worked the orchard until 1943. The Boughton family have long been synonymous with Mountain Lagoon. The family first purchased land in 1883 although Samuel Boughton Snr stayed in Richmond and was an alderman on Council in the 1870s and 1880s. He was also responsible for penning his memoirs published in the *Hawkesbury Herald* from 1902 to 1904, entitled 'Reminiscences of Richmond' under the pseudonym Cooramill. His son Sam Boughton Jnr went to Hawkesbury Agricultural College in 1904 and 1905. Sam married and settled at Mountain Lagoon in the home aptly named Cooramill. Sam Jnr died in 1961. There is a lovely avenue of trees that is called Sam's Way which includes a memorial.

Timber was an important early industry in Mountain Lagoon. Wattlebark was collected for use in the tanning industry, blue gum and hardwoods were milled as well as pulpwood. Some of the sawpits survived to the 1950s. John Anderson of Bell owned a sawmill in Mountain Lagoon around 1909. Root crops, corn and oats for horses were grown and citrus and apples were also key money makers.

During the 1950s, Mervyn Kennedy subdivided his 100 acre property creating smaller holdings and the population began to grow. The first official mail service commenced in 1957 with

Harry Nuzum as contractor. He delivered the mail for 15 years and then Joyce Dutch carried out the duties. Following this subdivision the Mountain Lagoon Road was upgraded.

Mount Tomah

The area surrounding Mount Tomah is fertile basalt soil. The region was originally called Fern Tree Hill but was known as Mount Tomah by the early 1820s. George Caley was one of the early explorers trying to cross the mountains west of the settlement. He arrived in NSW in 1804 collecting botanical specimens on behalf of Sir Joseph Banks and described the environment. In 1804 he arrived at Mount Tomah and camped there for four days. He went as far as Mount Banks and named it. As a botanist, the vegetation fascinated him and he compiled copious notes and sketches of the area. Early explorers were hampered by the deep gorges and Caley called the Grose, 'The Devil's Wilderness'.

The majority of Mount Tomah was a 1280 acre grant made to Susannah Bowen in 1830, the

ABOVE:
Wilton Stewart was the son of John Stewart of Mountain Lagoon. (BC HCCLS)

OPPOSITE PAGE ABOVE:
A bullock team pulling a truck up hill, Mountain Lagoon. (BC HCCLS)

OPPOSITE PAGE BELOW:
The Stewart family and a slab hut shed at Mountain Lagoon in the early 1900s. (BC HCCLS)

RIGHT:
Logging the forest giants was big business in Mt Tomah in the 1920s. (HCCLS)

ABOVE:
Arthur Hart and Ken Hungerford with a giant tree
at Mt Tomah.
(BC HCCLS)

RIGHT:
In the bush at Mount Tomah.
(BC HCCLS)

mother of G. M. C. Bowen, associated with Berambing and Bowen Mountain. In 1836 Susannah returned to England leaving her son to dispose of her property. Some of the land was sold to Captain George Bartley in 1838. A smaller amount of neighbouring land was owned by G. M. C. Bowen acquired in 1842 and in 1861. Most of the land at Mount Tomah was in the hands of the Bowen family. Bowen's son sold all of the Mount Tomah properties to Major Philip Charley of Belmont. Charley had become extremely wealthy as a result of the discovery of silver and lead at Broken Hill. In 1927 Charley sold some of his Mount Tomah land to a company known as Jungle Limited which proposed to preserve the land in its natural state. The proposal failed and in 1934 the land reverted to Charley. This land was subdivided and subsequently sold to various owners including 28 hectares to Effie and Alfred Brunet. They established a cut flower nursery in 1934. On her husband's death in 1968, Effie bequeathed the property to the NSW Government for use by the Royal Botanic Gardens Sydney and it opened to the public as Mount Tomah Botanic Gardens in 1987. The Brunets also donated a small portion of land in the 1960s to the Mount Tomah Bushfire Brigade for their shed.

Bells Line of Road was rarely used. From its beginning was a track and often in poor condition. Prior to World War II a decision was made to improve the route west. It wasn't until the end of the war that the track was overhauled and completed by 1949.

Mulgrave

Mulgrave Place was the early name given to the Hawkesbury district and was used in land grants to describe the area known today as Windsor and Pitt Town. It is not known why it was called Mulgrave but it is most likely after the English statesman, Baron Mulgrave (1774-1792). When the railway line was extended between Blacktown and Richmond in 1864, Mulgrave was one of only four railway stations established. State Rail only recently demolished the old station buildings.

Mulgrave Station in the late 1800s. (HCCLS)

North Richmond

North Richmond was originally known as the village of Enfield. The name changed during the 19th century to avoid confusion with Enfield in Sydney's inner west.

In 1789 when Governor Arthur Phillip explored the Hawkesbury River, he climbed Richmond Hill. He reported that, 'there is a flat of six or seven miles between Richmond Hill and a break in the mountains.' By the mid 1790s settlers were residing in the area. The earliest grants at North Richmond date from 1796 and include Andrew Connelly, John Griffiths, Emanuel Perry, William Laine, John Ryan and George Mohun. In the early 1800s larger grants were given to Richard Rouse and Archibald Bell. In 1810 when Governor Lachlan Macquarie toured the settlement, his party visited Belmont the home of Archibald Bell. He recorded in his journal, '... [we] rode up the Hill to call on Mrs. Bell (the Wife of Lt. Bell of the 102d Regt.) who resides on her Farm on the summit of this beautiful Hill, from which there is a very fine commanding Prospect of the River Hawkesbury and adjacent Country.'

The church buildings in North Richmond included the Methodist Church, established in 1857. It was known as the Enfield Chapel and Reverend Watkin took the opening service and described the building as, '... a strong but plain structure large enough for the worshippers of the place and a great improvement on the former one'. Bishop Barker laid the foundation stone of St Philip's Anglican in 1859 with services commencing in 1860. The church and burial ground were consecrated in 1861.

A schoolhouse for Anglicans was completed in 1861. George Sanders was appointed there in

LEFT:
The Charley family at Belmont, North Richmond. (HCCLS)

OPPOSITE PAGE:
Belmont was the superb home Charley built. Originally the site of Archibald Bell's property, the land was purchased by Philip Charley in 1889. (HCCLS)

BELOW:
Travellers Rest Hotel circa 1900s. (HCCLS)

The Hawkesbury River crossing at North Richmond in 1900. (GPO ML SLNSW)

1867. He put up with a miserable residence with a kind of church for a schoolhouse. In 1871 the public school opened. There were other denominational and private schools at various times in North Richmond including the school run by Thomas Williams which catered for small children. Thomas Sullivan was a shopkeeper and ran a school in both Richmond and North Richmond. The public school opened in 1871.

In 1821 the Hawkesbury River was crossed at North Richmond by a punt close to the site of today's bridge. Mrs Faithfull and George Matcham Pitt ran the ferry. Cattle swam across the river but the sheep were put on the punt. The punt held about 180 sheep and the punt operator recalls taking as many as 5000 across in one day.

As the road through Richmond was the main thoroughfare west and thousands of people were tramping to the goldfields, it was urgent that a bridge to be constructed over the Hawkesbury River to replace the ferry. In 1857 the Richmond Bridge Company was formed. A wooden bridge was built, the first over the Hawkesbury River, and opened in 1860. The first toll charges were 1/4d for each sheep, lamb, pig or goat; 6d per horse and 2d per person. No tolls were charged on Sundays or for funeral parties. Continual floods weakened the bridge and a new bridge was planned in the early 1900s. Sir John See, the Premier of NSW, turned the first sod in 1904 and the new bridge opened with much pomp and ceremony the following year. Construction costs

were about £20,000 and it was designed to carry a railway line. In 1926 additions took place to the bridge to get the Richmond Kurrajong railway line across the river. It was then Australia's largest reinforced concrete bridge. In 1926 the line from Richmond to Kurrajong opened.

Early settlers made their own arrangements regarding the circulation of mail. Charlie Eather ran the post office at his hotel during the 1850s. The mailman usually left his horse on the Richmond side and caught the ferry across. Mr Thompson and Tom Cambridge of Windsor both delivered the mail. Richmond's water supply was established in 1892 when a reservoir was built at North Richmond. Since 1892 North Richmond has had reticulated water.

The Pansy steam train crossing the bridge at North Richmond in the 1920s. (HCCLS)

A hotel existed at North Richmond by the early 1830s and was ideal for travellers and drovers with stock, waiting for the punt. The Pack Horse opened in the early 1830s and John Town built the Woolpack on the same site holding the license from to the 1840s. The Enfield Inn of the 1840s was licensed to Daniel Dickens who had the Beehive Inn. The Traveller's Rest was licensed to Jane Cribb in 1874 and later to John T. Town. The Exchange is listed with Alexander Matheson in 1894. Laura Phipps was the last licensee when it closed in 1913. The Riverview was established by the 1930s and still operates.

It was recommended following a parliamentary enquiry that mounted military police be stationed at North Richmond in 1847. The magistrates in Windsor had previously given constables living in the North Richmond district certain responsibilities. Some of the early constables included Edward Merrick, Fred Williams and William Grainger. In 1891 a police station was established in an old cottage on Bells Line of Road. In 1910 a new police station, including a lock up, was approved and constructed at North Richmond. The station was closed in 1933 and the building was rented out to local policemen.

Several significant heritage items have survived in North Richmond including Sunnyside, the home of George Matcham Pitt and family. Belmont remained in the Bell family until 1849 when it was subdivided. The main property has had various owners and was eventually purchased by Philip Charley in 1889. Charley built the extravagant mansion, also known as Belmont, to replace the earlier homesteads. It cost £56,000 to build. The Duke of Windsor stayed there as a guest in 1927. In 1951 Belmont was purchased and is now used as St John of God hospital. Archibald Bell's tomb is located on a knoll at Belmont.

The pastime of playing polo was popular in the late 1890s at North Richmond. Apparently it was played most afternoons and riders such as Harry Skuthorpe, Fred Stewart, Messrs Kirwan, Lambert, Allan and the infamous Harry 'Breaker' Morant formed a club. The local newspaper in 1898 stated that qualities for a good polo player included 'a firm seat on horseback, a quick eye and tendency to chance it a bit.'

Oakville

Oakville is situated about 4.5 kilometres south of Pitt Town. The name comes from the number of she-oaks that grew along local watercourses. One of the first settlers in the area was John Clark in 1894 whose land was next to Oak Hollow, an area filled with she-oaks. He named his property Oakville.

In 1804, Governor King set aside land in the districts of Nelson, Wilberforce and Richmond Hill, which later became known as Pitt Town Common, Wilberforce Common and Ham Common. Each area is over 5000 acres and was to be used by the settlers to graze stock. Oakville was originally part of King's Common.

During the early 1890s the area known as Pitt Town Common was subdivided and a large tract of land was set aside where the Pitt Town Co-operative Labour Settlement was established in 1893. This eventually became Scheyville. In 1894 about 40 blocks, ranging from 35 to 50 acres were made available for sale. Another early settler was Frederick Wilhelm Hanckel, son of German migrants. Hanckel acted on advice from his brother-in-law's family, the Weise's, that the area had potential. Hanckel owned 196 acres at Oakville and he used to cart fruit by horse and dray to the railway station for transport to the Sydney. He was a keen apiarist. Hanckel Road is named in his memory and descendants still live at Oakville.

Other prominent landowners included Albert and Himmel Bocks (who came after World War I), Johnson, Ogden, Hession, Agst, Weise, Smith, Speet, Powe

and the Sander families. Some of these families are remembered in streets names. Old Stock Route Road was used to transfer cattle from the northern grazing lands, via Wisemans Ferry, to either Mulgrave Railway station or Riverstone Meatworks.

A request was made to establish a school in Oakville in 1897. The school opened in 1900 with David Johnston appointed as the first teacher. Livelihoods in the Oakville area were made from poultry farming and citrus orchards. There was also dairying, pig farming and later mushrooms. In 1922 the Poultry Farmers Association was formed and became the Oakville Progress Association. A local hall was constructed in 1926 on land donated by Charles Clark. This hall was pulled down in the 1970s and the area became known as Clark Reserve.

The site of historic Clare House was originally part of Andrew Thompson's estate known as Killarney, located alongside Killarney Chain of Ponds. Purchased by emancipist Edward Redmond, he constructed a two storey-house for his daughter Sarah and her husband John Scarvell. John and Sarah and their large family lived on this property from at least 1830 until 1875. Part of the house is presumed to have been built in Macquarie's time. Clare Crescent, the road leading to the house, takes its name from the property.

Peninsula, Windsor

This area known as the Peninsula or r Peninsula is at the confluence of South Creek and the Hawkesbury River. Early grantees in the vicinity included John Palmer and his son George. John Stogdell was an ex-convict farming the Peninsula by the late 1790s and managing the adjoining farm for Palmer. Stogdell received one of the first licences in the Hawkesbury in 1798 when he established the Bush Inn at his rough and ready hut.

John Tebbutt (1763-1844) arrived with his wife Ann and family as free settlers to NSW in 1801. They moved to Windsor and established themselves as farmers and storekeepers. John Tebbutt, the astronomer, was born in Windsor in 1834, the son of John Tebbutt (1794-1870) and Virginia nee Saunders. He developed a lifelong love of astronomy as a boy. John Tebbutt (1794-1870) purchased land at the Peninsula, Windsor, in 1842 and built Peninsula House, a two storey Georgian house, in 1845. Tebbutt discovered the Great Comet in 1861 and by 1863 he had constructed the first of several observatories on the family property. He won various awards and was acclaimed for his research. He published *Astronomical Memoirs* in 1908 and during his life compiled nearly 400 articles for publication. John Tebbutt died in 1916, aged 82 years. His funeral was one of the largest held in Windsor. He is buried in a vault he designed at St Matthew's Anglican Cemetery, Windsor. A pioneer in the field of astronomy and highly regarded internationally, a lunar crater on the moon was named in his honour in 1973 and in 1984 he featured on the $100 note. John Tebbutt, a direct descendant, still lives on the property today, which is open to the public.

Many Chinese migrated to Australia in search of gold during the 19th century. Some of these established themselves in town's enroute to the goldfields. There were many Chinese living in the Hawkesbury by the 1850s who were involved in productive market gardens, particularly around Cornwallis, Richmond Lowlands and Windsor. In 1855 Tuim-Tuim, a Chinese pauper, died in Windsor Hospital. There was a headstone in the cemetery marking the grave of Fong Tim Bow who died in 1929. The Chin Company and the Hong Bun Garden Co. operated businesses in Windsor and there were Chinese operating gardens at the Peninsula. A Chinese called Sam Kin aged 60 years, died in his sleep in 1919 and the notice in the local paper said he had lived at the Peninsula gardens 'for many years'. He was buried at St Matthew's Cemetery, Windsor. Chinaman's Hill was used to describe the area located on The Terrace in Windsor where it slopes down past New Street intersection as there were a number of Chinese market gardens in that location.

LEFT:
John Tebbutt and one of his earlier observatories at Windsor.
(HCCLS)

Pitt Town

By 1794 settlers were living on the fertile riverbanks between Pitt Reach on the Hawkesbury River and the offshoot of South Creek, known as Pitt Town Bottoms. Governor William Bligh (1754-1817) purchased land at Pitt Town shortly after his arrival in the colony. A number of oak trees were planted on the property for Mary Putland, Bligh's daughter. Known as Bligh's Oaks they were cleared by the late 1940s.

Macquarie named the locality in the Nelson district Pitt Town in memory of the talented William Pitt (1759-1806) the British Prime Minister who was involved in the planning of the colony. The new township was laid out in 1811. The following year Macquarie returned to survey the burial ground and streets and commented on the poor quality of the ground and the difficulties of the site's location. In 1815 the site of the township was moved to its present location.

Church services would have been conducted from at least 1810. In 1825 Rev Matthew Devenish Meares was appointed to administer to Wilberforce and Pitt Town. Services were conducted in the schoolhouse and chapel until the foundation stone for St James Anglican was laid in 1857. The church, designed by Edmund Blacket, was constructed from sandstone quarried at Longneck Lagoon, and consecrated in 1859.

Presbyterians originally worshipped at Ebenezer, or met at William Hall's home in Pitt Town. The punt across the river enabled the ministers to effectively service both parishes. Scots Church was built in 1862. In 1811, Thomas Gilberthorpe, a convict who had arrived on the *William Pitt* in 1792, became the first licensee in Pitt Town. Daniel Smallwood built and operated the Bird in Hand inn from 1825 until 1840.

RIGHT:
Vine Cottage, a small slab cottage in Pitt Town.
(HCCLS)

RIGHT:
Pitt Town Public School gardens 1936.
(Ted Books)

Pitt Town Wharf. (HCCLS)

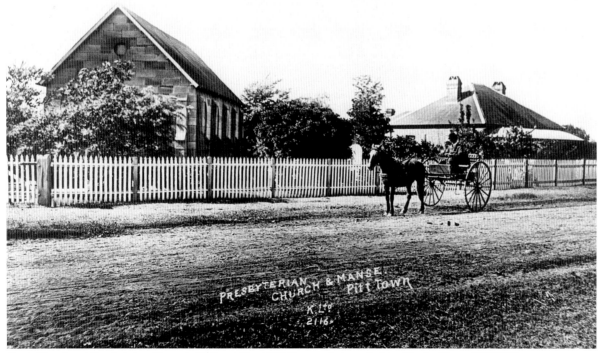

Scots Church and Presbyterian Manse in Bathurst Street Pitt Town, photographed by Charles Kerry. (HCCLS)

Surviving heritage items include Bona Vista, Bligh House, Strathmore, Vine Cottage and Huxley's blacksmith shop.

The Macquarie Arms in Bathurst Street was owned by Henry Fleming who was born in the colony. He conducted a hotel called the Blighton Arms but his licence was revoked in 1819 because he kept an 'irregular and riotous house'. Renamed the Macquarie Arms the licence was renewed in 1830. The adjacent house was called Mulgrave Place. Fortunately a large number of the famous Hawkesbury slab barns remain in the Pitt Town area, particularly along the Pitt Town Bottoms. Some of the now fragile barns were built in the first half of the 19th century and were used to store produce and stock.

A school was operating by 1814 and Matthew Thompson was listed as the first teacher. The building was a weatherboard not a permanent schoolhouse such as in Windsor, Wilberforce and Richmond. John Downing Wood, who arrived in 1811, was recorded as schoolmaster at Pitt Town by the 1820s and the school was suitably renovated to house a temporary chapel. By 1830 a new schoolhouse and chapel were constructed in Bathurst Street. A National School was run from 1861 until 1872 and there were various private and denominational schools. Pitt Town Public School was established in 1876 and a new school building opened in 1878. During the 1930s the School was known for its attractive gardens. The School of Arts opened in Bathurst Street in 1918.

By 1812 a punt operated between Wilberforce and Pitt Town. Other punts were constructed including the one built in 1828 by Captain John Grono who arrived as a boatswain in 1799 and was one of the finest shipbuilders in the Hawkesbury. He was involved in farming, real estate and the whaling and sealing industries.

Reverend McGarvie, the minister for Ebenezer Church, purchased a Georgian homestead built circa 1821 and owned the nearby punt for many years. The house became known as the Manse Farm and was the Presbyterian Manse for Ebenezer Church from 1826 until 1867. The punt service was discontinued in 1921. Reminders are Punt Road, Pitt Town and the Pitt Town Ferry Road on the Wilberforce side.

Some of the earliest settlers and pioneering families have connections here: families of John Bootle, a convict who arrived on the *Neptune* in 1790; Robert Hobbs who arrived in 1791 on the *Active*; James Wilbow, Daniel Smallwood and boatbuilder John Grono who came in 1799 on the *Buffalo*. In 1828 Laurence May and son Christopher Watkins May were the first to use irrigation pumps at Pitt Town Bottoms.

The marriage of Reverend George Macfie's daughter Mary to William Thomas Poole took place in 1867 with the reception at the Old Manse Farm in Bathurst Street. Floodwaters had never reached the farm and guests were not going to let a bit of rain get in the way of a celebration. Water surrounded the property and guests had to escape by boat, climbing out of an upstairs window. At nearby Percy Place everyone had left the property to attend the wedding except elderly William Hall and his carer, young James Butler. The waves of the flood were thrashing the stone walls and eventually James had to carry William to the safety of the barn. When they were rescued several hours later, they tied a valuable stallion to the boat. Another two horses followed the boat, swimming nearly three miles. One drowned but a draught horse was saved.

Pitt Town is currently under considerable pressure to develop as an urban centre and there has been extensive debate.

Richmond

When Governor Arthur Phillip visited the Richmond district in 1789 he described the soil as rich and suitable for cultivating crops. By 1794 a small community was established close to the present day township of Windsor. By the following year grants were being given out. The earliest grant was to William Rowe who was given 30 acres in 1795. Other grants soon followed.

Governor Lachlan Macquarie in 1810 recorded in his journal, 'the Township in the Richmond District I have named Richmond, from its beautiful situation, and as corresponding with that of its District.' He visited the township about a month after the naming ceremony and wrote, '...the scite [sic] of the church, schoolhouse and burying ground were marked out by strong posts ...The name of the town, painted on a board and nailed to a strong lofty post was put close to the beautiful bank immediately above and overlooking Pugh's Lagoon and adjoining rich lowlands where it is intended to erect the Church at Richmond.'

Although Brother Youl conducted the first

Alfred Meredith Woodhill and sons established a general store in Richmond in 1887. (HCCLS)

End of Boer War celebrations in Richmond 1903 and the view along Windsor Street. (HCCLS)

services in the Richmond district in 1808, it wasn't until 1810 that church services became more regular. A schoolhouse was erected at Richmond in 1813 and was used as a chapel on Sundays. Reverend Henry Fulton was appointed as second chaplain and he preached at Richmond and Castlereagh on alternate Sundays. The first schoolmaster appointed to Richmond was Matthew Hughes and he taught from 1813 until 1839. There were other denominational and private schools at various times in Richmond. Charles Hogsflesh kept a school in Richmond, as did Mr Travis and Mr McLean. Public education commenced in Richmond in 1860 with the opening of a National School in West Market Street. The building originally housed the Presbyterian school. The Richmond Public School eventually moved to premises in Windsor Street. It became a District Rural School between 1925 and 1954, teaching secondary classes. Richmond High School opened in 1955. The

School of Arts in Richmond was opened by the Premier Sir Henry Parkes in 1866. Richmond School of Arts is still used by the community and is the home of the Richmond Players, the local drama group which was established in 1952.

Although agriculture was the main industry in the Hawkesbury, shipbuilding was also important. Jonathan Griffiths was a prominent shipbuilder and his yards were located along the river just out of Richmond. His early vessels included the *Speedy* (1804) and the *Hazard* (1808). The *Elizabeth and Mary* was launched at Richmond Hill in 1810. The *Sydney Gazette* wrote, 'Her burthen [sic] is about 80 tons, her keel 48 feet, 18 feet beam; and is considered to be one of the handsomest vessels ever built in the colony.'

Mails were delivered three times per week from Windsor to Richmond from the 1820s. The post office was officially established in 1844 and the first postmaster appointed was William Edward Brew. In 1875 a single storey post office building was erected in Windsor Street. The first Telegraph Office opened in Richmond in 1867, nine years after the first line in Sydney. Richmond continued to expand and in the 1870s a police station and courthouse were built.

The Richmond Borough Council was incorporated in 1872. The election took place two months later with nine alderman elected to serve the area from Bourke Street to Pughs Lagoon.

ABOVE:
Sign of the Black Horse Hotel in Richmond was hung outside to advertise the hotel's name. (HCCLS)

RIGHT:
The Royal Hotel, on the corner of Windsor Street and East Market Street, Richmond 1879. (GPO ML SLNSW)

George Bowman was elected the first Mayor and Colonel C. S. Guest was the Town Clerk serving until 1901. Meetings were held in the School of Arts until 1913 when the site on the corner of March and West Market Streets was purchased and premises constructed. New chambers opened in 1940. Windsor and Richmond councils were amalgamated and formed Windsor Municipal Council at the beginning of 1949. The older buildings of Richmond Council Chambers in March Street are presently used to house the Hawkesbury City Band. The council offices house the Richmond Branch Library.

Hawkesbury Agricultural College was established on part of the Ham Common on the outskirts of Richmond in the 1890s. Commencing in 1891 alternative accommodation was found until the college buildings were functional in 1896. Courses were originally agriculturally related but it now forms part of the University of Western Sydney Hawkesbury where a wide range of subjects are taught.

Representative government was introduced in NSW in 1842. Robert Fitzgerald and William Bowman contested the seat of Cumberland that covered Windsor, Richmond, Campbelltown and Liverpool at the elections the following year. The main voting place in the Hawkesbury was at the courthouse in Windsor. That evening it was thought that Bowman was returned by a majority

ABOVE:
The Imperial Hotel was established in 1898 on the corner of March and East Market Streets in Richmond. The Imperial was demolished when the Richmond Inn was built in 1973. (HCCLS)

LEFT:
West Market Street from the intersection of March Street. (HCCLS)

The courthouse on the corner of Windsor Street and West Market Street, Richmond 1879. Note the old single storey post office in the background built in 1875 (GPO ML SLNSW)

Windsor Street towards West Market Street intersection, Richmond, after 1888 when the second storey was added to the post office plus the courthouse. (GPO ML SLNSW)

Flood rubbish pushes up against the Richmond bridge,
a wooden truss bridge for horse and carriage in 1879.
(GPO ML SLNSW)

Photographer Woodhill captures the scene of the Boer War soldiers setting off from Richmond Station in 1901. (HCCLS)

was built but the congregation outgrew the building and a larger building opened in 1842. The Paget Street building opened in 1929. The old site in the commercial centre of Richmond was sold and Kilduffs Buildings appeared in 1930. The chapel still remains and if you stand on the Richmond Park side of Windsor Street near the crossing you can see the original building with the inscription 'WESLEYAN CHAPEL 1842'.

Early Presbyterian services in Richmond were held in the homes of residents. George Bowman donated the land for a church in West Market Street and it was used for services by 1845. One of the most prominent of the ministers connected to this parish, was the Reverend James Cameron. He came to Richmond in 1856 and married George Bowman's daughter in 1857. He held some distinguished positions and was the Moderator of the Presbyterian Church of NSW in 1875 and 1901. The church tower, bell and the clock, later additions, were paid for by Bowman.

In 1848 it was suggested that a Catholic church be built. On the feast day of St Monica's in 1859 the church was opened by Father Terry. In 1878 a convent operated by the Good Samaritan nuns, and a school with boarding facilities, were constructed. The presbytery was built in 1899. The educating of students was of great consequence at St Monica's and the school expanded and grew to include secondary classes in 1944. In the 1940s the Poor Clare Nuns took over the convent and in the 1950s they assisted with teaching migrant children at Scheyville camp. A new church was built at St Monica's in 1982 although the old building still stands. Cardinal Edward Bede Clancy AC was born in Lithgow in 1923 and moved to Richmond where he attended St Monica's. In 1949 he was ordained into the Priesthood and celebrated his first mass at St Monica's. He was

of one vote and there was rioting in Windsor. Additional police had to be sent the following day and there were arrests made. Billy McAlpin apparently rode all night from the other side of the Bulga to give Bowman his vote. The crowd was so excited in Richmond that tables were brought out into the streets, singers were abundant and 'liquor flowed plentifully, and spirits ran high'. The votes were officially counted the next day and Bowman had won by four votes. The festivities carried on the next night as well with fireworks and music.

Richmond has many surviving historic sites and buildings including Toxana, Clear Oaks, Josieville, Benson House, Rutherglen, Andrew Town's house, Dr Cameron's known as Yulebah. Fine examples range from humble worker's cottages to Victorian residences. On the outskirts is Mountain View on Inalls Lane.

One of the earliest surviving homes in Australia is situated in the western end of Windsor Street. Bowman Cottage was purchased by George Bowman in 1818 from the previous owner, James Blackman. Bowman extended the brick-nog structure and there were eventually 12 rooms. He was a benefactor to the local Presbyterian Church and the first mayor of Richmond in 1872. The cottage was his home until his death in 1878. The building fell into disrepair but was purchased by the NSW Government and restored in the 1980s.

St Peter's Anglican Church (1839) was designed by Francis Clark and built by James Atkinson. The church has beautiful stained glass windows. There have been some minor additions over the years and the building, with the 1848 parsonage and the cemetery across the road, a backdrop of Pughs Lagoon and the Blue Mountains in the distance, is an appealing scene. In 1827 a Wesleyan Chapel

RIGHT:
Richmond railway station in the early 1950s with the Imperial Hotel to the left. The crossing had been necessary across East Market Street when the railway still extended to Kurrajong. The line officially closed in 1952.
(HCCLS)

OPPOSITE PAGE:
St Andrew's Presbyterian Church West Market Street, Richmond was built in 1845 by George Bowman. The tower was added in 1877. The school on the left was built in 1879, the year the photograph was taken.
(HCCLS)

BELOW:
Commissioning of the Richmond Sewerage Works 1962.
(HCCLS)

appointed Archbishop of Sydney in 1983 and created Cardinal Priest of the Holy Roman Church by Pope John Paul II in 1988 and retired in 2001.

Richmond Park was originally marked out as the market square in 1811 but has been mainly used for recreation. The grandstand or pavilion was built in 1883. Today there is concern for the fragile trees and surrounds and a conservation plan is investigating ways to protect the park.

Richmond's main commercial area is Windsor Street. Banks, offices and shops are located alongside churches and hotels. The Royal Hotel and Commercial Hotel survived the 20th century although modernised. A few older shops and the National Australia Bank appear in Windsor Street but many of the older commercial buildings have disappeared. Anyone with an interest in Richmond should read the memoirs of Alfred Smith and Samuel Boughton written in the 1900s.

Rickabys Creek

Rickabys Creek runs through the areas of Londonderry and Clarendon, entering the Hawkesbury River just west of Windsor between Argyle Reach and Windsor Reach. Thomas Rickerby or Rickaby was a convict who arrived in the colony in 1791 and was granted 30 acres of land in 1794 at the confluence of the Hawkesbury River and the creek that now bears his name. He was chief constable until 1804. He died in 1818 aged 67 and is buried at St Matthew's Anglican Cemetery in Windsor.

ABOVE:
Aerial view of the junction of Rickabys Creek and Hawkesbury River in a 1960s flood. (RAAF)

OPPOSITE PAGE ABOVE:
A view of Riverstone from along the railway near the Meatworks, in the late 1890s, was photographed by Charles Kerry.
(HCCLS)

OPPOSITE PAGE BELOW:
The opening of the electrified line to Riverstone was a cause of celebration on the 18.5.1975.
(SRA SRNSW)

LEFT:
The bridge over Rickabys Creek photographed by the Government Printer in 1879. (GPO ML SLNSW)

Riverstone

The site of Riverstone was originally part of a 2500 acre grant given to Lieutenant-Colonel Maurice O'Connell in 1810 on his marriage to Mary Putland, the daughter of Governor William Bligh. O'Connell gave it the name of Riverston after an affiliation with a place in Ireland but it was mistakenly misspelt in the 1860s and subsequently known as Riverstone. The grant covered the area between Bandon and Windsor Roads, Garfield Road and Eastern Creek. O'Connell left the colony for a period and the land was leased but following his return some of the property was subdivided and sold after 1840. Following O'Connell's death in 1856, the remaining estate was subdivided and sold at auction.

In 1864, the railway line passed through with a

station and a small village developing around it. Benjamin Richards began the Riverstone Meatworks in 1878. He was involved in the butchery business and owned large tracts of cattle properties all over NSW. He purchased land adjacent to the railway line in Riverstone and construction of the meatworks began. The Riverstone Meatworks was extremely successful until the early 1990s when, following large losses, the business closed in 1994. Some employees were the third and fourth generation descendants of original workers. The Riverstone Public School opened in 1883 and the High School in 1962. Religious services commenced with the establishment of St Paul's Anglican Church in 1883, St Andrew's Presbyterian in 1888 and St John's Catholic Church in 1904. Some of Riverstone originally came under the jurisdiction of Windsor Council but was transferred to Blacktown Council in 1928.

Sackville

Sackville was named after Viscount Sackville who was the British Secretary of State in 1776. Sackville is divided by the Hawkesbury River and includes the Cumberland Reach, Kent Reach, Sackville Reach and Portland Reach along the river. Centred around Sackville Reach, the area to the north is now known as North Sackville, whilst the area around Sackville Ferry is known as Sackville. 1823 saw the opening of a school at Sackville Reach therefore most of the

Ferry at Sackville in the 1930s. (HCCLS)

Hawkesbury settlers had access to educational facilities. During these days it was not uncommon for school children to have to row across the river in order to attend school.

At the northern end of Sackville Reach stand two sandstone churches on either side of the river. Church services were first held at Sackville Reach in 1833 and in 1839 a church was planned. By 1861 funds were available and St Thomas Anglican was completed but the great flood of 1867 swept the church away. A stone obelisk marks the site within the grounds of the Sackville Cemetery. A new site was found on higher ground and the church was consecrated in 1874. This church was gutted by fire in 1959 and later restored in 1960.

On the other side of the river stands the Methodist Church at North Sackville. This church was built in 1869 replacing an earlier building destroyed in the 1867 flood. It closed in 1955 and was used as a church camp until 1987. It is now in private hands as is the nearby manse built in 1879.

There were several wharves along this section of the river including Fiaschi's wharf at the northern end of Portland Reach. The most well known wharf was Churchill's Wharf, a major port

Churchill's Wharf at Sackville was used to load produce onto riverboats. (Tizzana Winery)

Winter time at Tizzana Vineyard at Sackville Reach in 1889. (Tizzana Winery)

Scheyville

The first subdivisions of Pitt Common were in the early 1890s. Some 930 hectares were set aside and the Pitt Town Co-operative Labour Settlement was established in 1893. Like a commune, camps were established to provide alternative employment during the 1890s depression but folded after several years. In 1896 the site was set up as the Casual Labour Farm to provide employment and temporary accommodation for unemployed and homeless men. During the early 1900s a training program for boys was established but the Casual Labour farm closed and the farm concentrated on training agricultural labourers. The site then became the Government Agricultural Training Farm and was used as part of the Dreadnought Scheme. About 7500 teenage boys from Britain arrived in Australia between 1910 and 1939 to gain experience as agricultural labourers. Most of the boys were sent to the farm at Pitt Town, known as Scheyville after Francis William Schey, the Director of Labour in NSW. The district eventually took the name Scheyville.

In 1910 up to 100 boys could be accommodated and the farm was flourishing with wheat, oats, maize, potatoes and other crops. The students learned most aspects of farming life including shearing, dairying and first hand experience with sawmilling, blacksmithing and saddlery. During World War I the superintendent was responsible for persons classed as 'prisoners' from countries at war with Australia. At the beginning of the war there were over 200 men and boys as well as 87 German prisoners. During World War II, Scheyville was occupied by the army and used by the 1st Parachute Battalion and several artillery units.

of call for the larger steamers when siltation of the Hawkesbury became an issue in the 1880s. It was during this period that the idea of extending the railway from Mulgrave to Sackville was advanced but the project never eventuated. A ferry service commenced in 1883 next to Churchill's Wharf with a small hand operated punt. This was replaced in 1930 by a power driven punt.

Italian born Dr Thomas Henry Fiaschi was appointed surgeon at the Windsor Hospital in 1876. He pioneered Listerian surgical techniques. At Sackville Reach, Dr Thomas Fiaschi first planted vines in 1882. Over subsequent years a purpose built winery and residence were erected and Tizzana Vineyards was officially established in 1887. Fiaschi hired many local Aborigines from the Sackville Reach Aborigine Reserve, and Italian immigrants, to work at Tizzana.

Dr Fiaschi was involved with the military and during his life went on to become a highly decorated and respected surgeon with the NSW Army Medical Corps. Visitors to Tizzana Vineyards can enjoy wine from the cellar door and take in some of the history by viewing items on display.

Fiaschi continued with his wine business until his death in 1927, at which time his second wife Amy kept the operations going. In 1955, the cellars were broken into by vandals and set on fire leaving just a sandstone shell. 1969 saw the restoration of the ruins by Peter and Carolyn Auld with vineyards being replanted in 1980. The Aulds are still in residence today.

Government Agricultural Training Farm at Scheyville circa 1912. (SLNSW)

After the war and the flood of migrants to Australia, the camp was used as a Migrant Accommodation Centre between 1949 and 1964. Following time at Scheyville migrant camp, a large number of these migrants settled in the Hawkesbury district. They included people from Macedonia, Greece, Italy, Poland, Germany and Malta. Some of them became market gardeners, others were involved in other commercial enterprises in the district.

In the mid 1960s part of the estate at Scheyville was auctioned off in two to four hectare residential blocks. For the next few years Scheyville operated as an Officer Training Unit. The men on National Service were trained as infantry platoon commanders expressly for Vietnam jungle warfare. With the end of National Service in 1967, the unit closed.

Over the last 30 years, the site has had several uses but remained empty for some time. Some of the proposals included a prison complex, an airport, a rubbish tip and housing development. In 1996 the Scheyville National Park was created covering 920 hectares. This park now conserves the woodland ecosystems and the endangered ecological communities of this area. It also safeguards the existing buildings that form the history of Scheyville over the last century. Longneck Lagoon Field Studies Centre, specialising in environmental education for school students, forms part of the Scheyville National Park.

South Creek

South Creek, one of the smaller tributaries of the Hawkesbury, was the location of the first European settlement. Lieutenant-Governor Major Grose in a message on the 29 April 1794 states he had placed 22 settlers on the banks of the Hawkesbury River. These farms were 30 acres each and situated between Pitt Reach and the South Creek tributary. South Creek is now known by its Aboriginal name Wianamatta.

Permission was granted to Andrew Thompson to charge a toll for the use of his 'floating bridge' over South Creek as of 1802. In 1805 the structure was damaged by lightning and needed repair. In 1811 a higher level bridge was built and renamed Howe Bridge when opened in 1813 by Governor Lachlan Macquarie. The *Sydney Gazette* reported an earthquake in 1823, 'The town of Windsor was greatly shakened by the noise of something like an earthquake, accompanied by trembling of the earth … inhabitants were so terribly alarmed … discovered that Howe Bridge, supposed to be one of the finest bridges in the Colony had actually fallen in.'

A new bridge was constructed, opening in 1853. This bridge had laminated timber arches and was called the Fitzroy Bridge. It was replaced in 1881 with an iron bridge replaced again with a higher level bridge in 1976. The Windsor Flood Evacuation Route was announced in 2003. This should provide an evacuation route when there is a flood.

There was a toll house recorded on an 1816 map of Windsor however little information survives. Tenders were called for a toll house to be erected in 1834 and the building was completed in 1835. Unfortunately the building was practically demolished in the 1864 flood when it shifted off its foundations. It was rebuilt with some alterations shortly after. The Toll House at South Creek is one of only two intact toll houses remaining in NSW. The other is at Mt Victoria. It is a small building with a bay window from which the toll keeper could see the road. The toll was abolished by the Windsor Road Trust in 1887. In 1975 a new high level bridge was constructed over South Creek almost concealing the Toll House from view. The exterior of this quaint reminder of the past can be viewed from beside the Fitzroy Bridge. 'Jack the Barber' operated his barber shop at the Toll House in the early 19th century. His billboard advertised:

> To all who has hair or beards to crop,
> I recommends my shaving shop,
> Neatly and deftly I can trim,
> the roughest beard on any chin,
> I cuts the hair on the newest plan,
> And charges little nor any man'

Jack also held the record for catching the largest eel in South Creek. It weighed 20 pounds!

ABOVE:
Fitzroy Bridge, built with laminated timber arches, opened in 1853. It was replaced with an iron bridge in 1881. (HCCLS)

RIGHT:
The toll house at South Creek, Windsor. (HCCLS)

A view of South Creek in flood in the 1960s. The toll house is in the left hand corner and the small settlement at McGraths Hill, including the silos, can be seen in the top right hand corner. (RAAF)

South Windsor

Part of Governor Macquarie's original design for Windsor was in the area south of the railway line. Selected portions were granted but not developed by the owners. These were later resumed and made available for purchase in the 1850s and 1860s. In the 1880s the area became known as Newtown but became South Windsor in the 20th century.

Situated at the southern end of the town was the Presbyterian Cemetery, appropriated in 1833. Also located at the south of the township was William Cox's property Fairfield which had been granted to his son Henry in 1804. The house was owned or leased by various occupants including the Hale's and their grandson Henry McQuade who extended the house in the 1880s to accommodate his prosperous lifestyle.

In South Windsor in the 1850s some property was subdivided and sold but the extension of the railway line to Richmond resumed land for the track. The railway opened in 1864 and effectively divided the town in two. The track had to be crossed to get to Newtown.

Brickfield Hill was an area, east of Mileham Street where local brick making took place in the 1860s. When George Carroll's tannery at Newtown came onto the market Richard Cobcroft was quick to purchase and extend the business. By 1888 the tannery had 23 pits and was producing 120 hides per week. In 1882, James and son Walter Mullinger constructed a shop adjacent to their house. It was operated by various family members as a small general store from the 1880s until it closed in the 1970s. The Cobcroft family extended their six room cottage to a 14 room stylish villa by the mid 1890s. Renamed Glenroy the house included a ballroom and billiard room.

ABOVE:
Fairfield House originally built by William Cox and extended by Henry McQuade in the 1880s was used as a reception venue in the 1970s. (HCCLS)

ABOVE RIGHT:
A shop at South Windsor in the 1890s. (HCCLS)

The Speedway was opened in 1949 by Windsor RSL on land owned by the Windsor Council in the area enclosed by Mileham and Argyle Streets and Fairey Road. A crowd of about 2000 spectators watched motorcycles, sidecar and speed cars race. Jack Brabham, later a Formula 1 World Champion, raced on the circuit. It closed in 1950 but was reopened in 1955 for stock-car racing and for hot rods in the 1960s, finally closing in 1967.

RIGHT:
Windsor Railway Station in 1880 with the original railway gates across the track to South Windsor. The underpass came later. (SRA SRNSW)

Tennyson

Tennyson is a small settlement located in the Currency Parish, about 5 kilometres north east of North Richmond. It was also known as Sallys or Salis Bottoms but the name was changed to Tennyson in the mid 1890s. By 1894 the local paper reported Sallys Bottoms was now called Tennyson. As the community was relatively small, only a provisional school was warranted. The community supplied the building and the classes commenced in 1895. It became a public school in 1900, closing in 1951.

RIGHT:
Tennyson public school circa 1912. (Marj Clarke)

BELOW:
Joe Wilson, inside the car in 1955, owned the Rivoli Theatre for a period. (Alan Strachan)

Vineyard

Vineyard is located 2.5 kilometres north of Riverstone. They were originally part of the grant to Lieutenant-Colonel Maurice O'Connell on the occasion of his marriage to Mary Putland nee Bligh in 1810 by Governor Macquarie. When the O'Connells left the colony in 1814 the land was leased but following their return 20 years later some of the property was subdivided and sold. With O'Connell's death in 1856 the remaining estate was subdivided and sold at auction. Vineyards were established and gave the locality its name. It was also known as The Vineyards. The grapes were destroyed during the phylloxera outbreak in the late 1880s which swept through the Sydney district.

The first road which follows along Old Hawkesbury Road and is the original road that ran between the Hawkesbury and Parramatta, was built in 1794. The Beehive Coaching Inn was built by James Barnett in 1848 and is located on Windsor Road. It was run by James Strachan (1811–1876) from about 1848 to 1858. His descendants still live at Vineyard.

Vineyard is situated on the railway line between Riverstone and Windsor. The line opened in 1864. In 1935 a platform and shelter shed were constructed. The community had to guarantee materials and labour. A provisional school opened in 1872. In 1880 the school became Vineyard Public School and moved to its present site.

St Andrew's Anglican Hall at Vineyard was officially opened in 1932 with a market fete and dance. The following year local identity Mr Rannard set about erecting a Public Hall at Vineyard which opened in 1933, adjacent to the shop that housed the post office. There were dances held here every Saturday night and large crowds of young people regularly attended. This hall was used from 1946 as The Rivoli, a cinema with seating for 200. The first movie shown was the epic *Gone with the Wind*. The Rivoli closed in 1958.

Webbs Creek

Webbs Creek, a tributary of the Hawkesbury River, is near Bathurst Reach and is less than two kilometres below the Macdonald River confluence. James Webb arrived free on the *Scarborough* in 1790 and owned a large tract of land here. Many of the early inhabitants were involved in farming and used the river for transport. Some of the original settlers included members of the Books, Rose, Reilly, Butler, Sullivan and Douglass families.

Alexander Books arrived free in 1791 onboard the *Active*, skilled in sealing, shipbuilding and eventually farming. In 1809 he was stranded in the wilderness of New Zealand whilst sealing. Books and crew were marooned off the South Island of New Zealand for four years and were rescued by Captain John Grono in 1813 on the ship *Governor Bligh*. In due course, Alexander Books married Grono's daughter Margaret in 1819 and they began a large family, with many descendants still living in the district. Books eventually settled at Webbs Creek, although the family was synonymous with Pitt Town and Portland Head. As well as farming the Books family were boatbuilders. In 1832 he owned the schooner *Caledonia* and he also built the *Highland Lass* and the *Margaret* during the 1840s. At the time of his death in 1864 he owned over 300 hectares at Webbs Creek, including Webb's original grant.

During the 1978 flood the Webbs Creek ferry broke its moorings and collided with the two ferries from Wisemans Ferry that were secured downstream. The impact resulted in three ferries

LEFT:
View of Webbs Creek in 1910. (HCCLS)

being swept down the Hawkesbury River with three ferrymen onboard the largest one. The Webbs Creek punt was finally tied up near Haycock Reach whilst the vessels from Wisemans Ferry came to rest near Courangra Point almost 20 kilometres from their original position. The following day the two ferries at Courangra, with the men still aboard, were on the loose again. Despite being met by tugs and other safety vessels the ferries were out of control, towing masses of flood debris and heading for the bridge at Brooklyn. There were fears for the bridge pylons and it seemed the only course was to scuttle the ferries but fortunately they finally came aground near Peat Island and were secured to the shore.

Wilberforce

Wilberforce is located on the banks of the Hawkesbury River, about 7 kilometres north of Windsor. The surrounding fertile floodplains were sought after early on. One of Macquarie's 1810 Five Towns, he recorded, '…the Township for the Phillip District; on the North or left Bank of the Hawkesbury, I have named Wilberforce — in honor of and out of respect to the good and virtuous William Wilberforce, British Member of Parliament and humanitarian a true Patriot and the real Friend of Mankind'. Early in 1811 Macquarie returned with James Meehan, the surveyor to mark out the township.

James Kenny established a school at Wilberforce in 1807. Governor Macquarie visited in 1813 and surveyed the site for a schoolhouse and chapel. This temporary building was completed the following year. The current schoolhouse, started in 1819 and, constructed from brick and limewash, was built by Captain John Brabyn who was originally in the NSW Corps. In later years he settled at York Lodge in Windsor and was a magistrate. Macquarie originally established four schoolhouses in the Hawkesbury but Wilberforce, completed in 1820, is the only surviving structure. The first headmaster at Wilberforce Public School was Thomas Taylor and until 1907 students of all ages were taught in the same room. The present day School of Arts hall in Wilberforce was officially opened in 1930. After World War II the School of Arts was used to screen movies.

Wilberforce Common was established by Governor King in 1804 and was used by the community to graze stock. In the 1890s a camp, Copeland Village, was established on the common. Like a commune, the camp provided alternative employment during the 1890s depression.

Reverend Robert Cartwright was the resident minister for the Hawkesbury from 1810. Services were held on alternate Sundays in the schoolhouse. In 1846 a meeting was held to discuss the establishment of a church. A plan was prepared by architect Edmund Blacket and St John's Anglican was consecrated in 1859.

A feature at St John's is the vertical sundial. The year of consecration is cut into the wall and the initials 'J W' (John Wenban who made the sundial). John Wenban was the schoolteacher between 1842 and 1859, as well as the parish clerk. He was killed accidentally when he was thrown from a horse drawn cart later that year and is buried at Wilberforce Cemetery.

Books family of Webbs Creek were renowned boatbuilders. (HCCLS)

Gathering at the Wilberforce Schoolhouse in 1920. (HCCLS)

The earliest surviving headstone at Wilberforce cemetery belongs to Margaret Chaseling who died in 1815. Matthew James Everingham, who arrived with the First Fleet, died in 1817 has a unique epitaph the first lines reading 'Farewell vain world I have had anough of thee.' Many of their descendants still live in the Hawkesbury. Unfortunately the cemetery has been vandalised in the last few years and hopefully the recently commenced 'Friends' group will help protect it.

A poignant headstone which was once located on the banks of the Hawkesbury River in Wilberforce, was relocated to the grounds of the historic school house by the Hawkesbury Historical Society in 1960.

> In memory of *JOHN HOWORTH*
> *who departed this life*
> *October 8th 1804. Aged 11 years*
> *it was the subtile serpent's bite he cride*
> *then like a rose bud cut he drup'd and died*
> *in life his Fathers glorey*
> *and his mothers pride*

In 1856 the first post office was approved. Maria Buttsworth was postmistress in 1890 followed by her daughter Mrs L. Daley in 1912. Her granddaughter Gwen Tuckerman took over in 1952 with great-granddaughter Jill Vincent running it from 1975 to 1985. The telephone was connected to Wilberforce in 1891. A Scout Hall was built at Wilberforce by voluntary labour, behind the Colo Shire Council Chambers in 1933. It was reported to be the first scout hall built in the Hawkesbury.

The Australiana Pioneer Village in Wilberforce was established by the late Bill McLachlan. It is listed on the State Heritage Inventory as a significant item. Dugald Andrew 'Bill' McLachlan purchased the property in the 1960s with a dream

Australia Day celebrations in 1988 at Australiana Pioneer Village. About 3000 visitors enjoyed the festivities at Wilberforce. *(HCCLS)*

of rescuing some of the Hawkesbury's heritage. He transferred a number of historic buildings that were at risk during the 1970s. Many would have been demolished. His vision was to create a recreational park on the riverbank that would also have some educational and historical purpose.

The most significant is Rose Cottage, believed to be Australia's oldest surviving timber building, built circa 1811. The cottage was constructed by Thomas Rose (1749-1833) who arrived on the *Bellona* in 1793 as one of the first free settlers in the colony. Amongst the resited buildings are the stables from the Black Horse Inn, Richmond, Kurrajong Railway Goods Shed and Bowd's Sulky Shed from Wilberforce. Bill McLachlan died in 1971 aged 54 years and is buried in the grounds of the village. The site, currently owned by Hawkesbury Council, is leased. Operated by Friends of Australiana Pioneer Village, it reopened in 2011.

District constables were appointed to Wilberforce from the 1820s. A lock up existed from at least the 1830s and a police station was opened in 1883. In 1906 a provisional council was elected to co-ordinate local government in the Colo area. John Lamrock (first president) plus Edward Bowd, Henry Wilson, William Gosper, Arthur Anderson and James McMahon were duly elected. The first Colo Council met in 1906 in a rented room at Wilberforce. New council chambers and offices opened in 1910. In 1981, Windsor and Colo Councils amalgamated to form Hawkesbury Shire Council. This building at Wilberforce has been the Control Centre for Hawkesbury's Rural Fire Services for some time.

ABOVE:
The township of Wilberforce late last century. (HCCLS)

LEFT:
Aerial view of Wilberforce 1958. (HCCLS)

Windsor

Windsor is located about 53 kilometres north west of Sydney and is one of the oldest European settlements in Australia. By 1794, Grose settled people on South Creek. When Governor Macquarie visited the Green Hills a settlement had already been established on the high ground adjacent to the Hawkesbury River. Focussing around the wharf, the granary, schoolhouse and other buildings were established around what is now known as Thompson Square. Green Hills officially became known as Windsor in 1810. Macquarie named Windsor after the town in England.

When Macquarie departed for England in 1820 the town had a feeling of permanence with public buildings including the military barracks. The first garrison had been stationed in Windsor since 1795. In 1817, a barrack building was constructed on the site of the present day police station in Bridge Street. Other buildings were added at various stages. Several different regiments were stationed at Windsor during the 1800s. Officers were billeted at the Macquarie Arms which was leased as Officers' quarters and mess. The military had a presence in Windsor until 1848. In 1924 the old barracks were demolished and new buildings constructed. Part of the perimeter wall still exists. Transportation of convicts to NSW was

By 1820 Windsor had a feeling of permanence with many public buildings. In 1879 Macquarie's vision for this town had developed. (GPO ML SLNSW)

Convent at Windsor 1879. (GPO ML SLNSW)

Windsor School in 1879 looking up George Street, towards Dight Street. (GPO ML SLNSW)

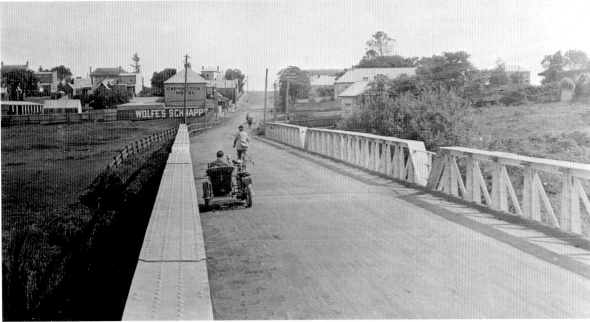

terminated in 1840. Four years later the *Hawkesbury Courier* complained that the stocks 'relics of the dark ages' in Bridge Street should be removed immediately.

As the river silted up and the prosperous river trade declined, the commercial centre shifted south towards the railway which was established in 1864. The main businesses in the town were related to agriculture. There were saddlery and harness making businesses, tanneries, several shoemakers. newspapers, banks, legal firms as well as grocery stores. On the outskirts were distilleries and breweries, cordial makers, brick makers, coach and wagon building and boat building businesses.

In 1874, the township of Windsor suffered a huge calamity. A fire started in a tannery near New Street and burned almost everything in its path up George Street to the Fitzgerald Street intersection and back down Macquarie Street. There was one fatality and very little salvaged from the ruins. The fire covered about 12 hectares and destroyed 53 buildings, including 36 homes, in a single afternoon. Little was covered by insurance and it took many years for the community to recover. The Wesleyan Hall in Macquarie Street, adjacent to today's Coles car park is one of the few surviving buildings.

Reverend Robert Cartwright was appointed to the Hawkesbury as Chaplain in 1810. In 1814 a schoolhouse and chapel were built near

ABOVE:
Windsor School of Arts in Bridge Street Thompson Square 1879. This building was used as a public hall and a library.
(GPO ML SLNSW)

LEFT:
Bridge Street from South Creek circa 1920s.
(HCCLS)

George Street, Windsor 1879, from Fitzgerald Street looking down to the railway. Many of these buildings were built after the fire that destroyed much of George and Macquarie Streets in 1874.
(GPO ML SLNSW)

Thompson Square. Three years later the foundation stone for St Matthew's Anglican Church was laid by Governor Lachlan Macquarie. Designed by ex-convict Francis Greenway, it is considered his masterpiece. The building was consecrated in 1822 by Rev Samuel Marsden. The rectory was built by William Cox and completed by 1825. The first public mass in the Hawkesbury was held in 1803 but it was not until 1831 that

Father Dowling was appointed as the first Catholic priest. St Matthew's Catholic Church opened in 1840. The Anglican and Catholic churches, located across the park from each other, have the same name. The reason for this is not known.

A Presbyterian Church was established in 1843 and the Congregational Church built in 1869. A Wesleyan chapel was established in 1818 and

replaced in 1839. A hall opened adjacent in 1861 and was used as a school. This church was burned down in 1874 but was replaced 1876.

The first liquor licenses were distributed in the Hawkesbury shortly after settlement and by the 1840s there were many public houses including the Help Me Through the World. In the 1850s there were 17 hotels listed in Windsor. The hotels were also social meeting places and were used for

auctions, travelling dentists, inquests and public meetings. Entertainment was not limited to the adults. A merry-go-round was conducted at the John Young Hotel in Thompson Square. The first circus in Windsor was run by Black Jones at the rear of Miss Bushell's Hotel. The first waxworks show was held in the same building in the 1870s.

The Macquarie Arms requires a specific mention as it is the oldest building used as a hotel in Australia, although not licensed continuously. Constructed in 1815 by Richard Fitzgerald, it was used by the military in the 1830s and then as a residence. It re-opened as the Royal Hotel in 1873 and was renamed the Macquarie Arms in 1961.

A post office was officially operating in Windsor by 1828. A telegraph station was established in 1860 and Windsor could communicate with the outside world during the time of flood. The first locally produced newspaper was the *Windsor Express* in 1843. The longest running is the *Windsor and Richmond Gazette* which started in 1888 and is now the *Hawkesbury Gazette*.

The Borough Council of Windsor was incorporated in 1871 and Robert Dick was elected mayor. Meetings were held in the

ABOVE:
View down George Street towards the railway from the intersection of Kable Street.
(Charles Kerry photo, HCCLS)

LEFT:
Many of these wonderful verandahs were removed in the 1950s. George Street at the turn of the century. Johnston Street is on the right.
(Charles Kerry photo, HCCLS)

George Street, Windsor.

R. A. Pye (copyright)

George Street Windsor from Fitzgerald Street intersection looking towards Thompson Square. The Fitzroy Hotel is on the left. The two girls on the right are apparently the photographer's daughters. (HCCLS)

ABOVE:
Cart loads of watermelons queue near Windsor Public School in George Street waiting to unload produce at Windsor Railway Station circa 1890s. (Ted Books)

LEFT:
View of George Street Thompson Square from Bridge Street, Windsor. (HCCLS)

Oddfellows Hall until new premises were purchased in George Street in 1891. In 1966, a new complex was constructed in George Street. This has been extended several times to accommodate its growth. Colo and Windsor Councils amalgamated in 1981 and became Hawkesbury City Council in 1989.

In Windsor is the acclaimed Thompson Square which includes the Macquarie Arms, the Doctors House and Hawkesbury Museum, Crescentville, Sunnybrae and Loder House. Around North Street and the courthouse are Trevallyn, Claremont Cottage, Mrs Cope's Cottage and Fitzroy Cottage. The old general store at 394 George Street has splendid carvings by O'Kelly. Some very fine brick cottages and terrace houses are in this street.

The old Windsor Hospital in Macquarie Street started out as a convict barracks built in 1820. In 1823 it was converted to a hospital. The hospital was given to the people of Windsor in 1846 after the end of convict transportation. The elderly and poor as well as those needing treatment for diseases were treated in the hospital. The Hawkesbury Benevolent Society raised funds to operate it and some of the paupers were expected to assist with light duties and work in the vegetable garden otherwise they may lose 'their allowance of tea, sugar and tobacco'.

In 1899 a Royal Commission into hospitals concluded that all of the Windsor buildings were in very poor condition and the hospital 'has throughout, the old peculiar poor-house smell and in its present condition [the building is] inherently unfit for hospital purposes.' Eventually the old buildings were extensively modernised and the new renovations opened in 1911. The hospital underwent many more changes throughout the

Cricket was a popular sport in the Hawkesbury. (WC ML SLNSW)

A charabanc carries a group of tourists on a rural outing to the Hawkesbury district in 1928. (GPO ML SLNSW)

20th century. In the 1990s a new hospital was built on the opposite side of the road. Hawkesbury City Council renovated the old hospital to its 1911 appearance and leases the building. A library and art gallery complex, the Deerubbin Centre, was constructed on part of the site.

In the catastrophic floods in 1867 the town was divided into several islands with only portions above water including a section of Thompson Square and along The Terrace to the park. In 1896, one of the most bizarre accidents to take place in Windsor was when Jessie Toomey was struck by lightning. She was talking to Mrs Dodd, a friend in the doorway of a house in Macquarie Street, when a severe thunderstorm struck. Jessie had several metallic curlers in her hair and was

killed instantly. Mrs Dodd was knocked unconscious and received a nasty gash on the head.

It was during the Boer War that the controversial event involving larrikin and Lieutenant Harry Harbord Morant, known as 'The Breaker', occurred. He was court martialled and convicted for murdering Boer prisoners. He was shot by a firing squad in 1902. Morant was a skilful horseman and lived in the Hawkesbury during the 1890s. He was employed at North Richmond and his antics were often reported in the newspaper. In 1898 he was recorded as jumping a gelding over a seven foot paling fence near the old Clarendon hotel. Using his pen name 'The Breaker' he also wrote poems, some published by the *Bulletin*. He sent the following

prophetic letter to J. J. L. Fitzpatrick, editor of the *Windsor and Richmond Gazette*. 'Hope you're well. I'm on active service out here. Not bad fun, but no sheets nor servants … have not dropped across Banjo Paterson or any of the NSW crowd yet. 'Gawd' knows when I'll see any old Hawkesbury fellows again–probably when we wear a halo. I'm in the Mounted Rifles, and perchance may get a stray bullet when out scouting. But the Boers and d—- bad shots. Their marksmanship is huge fable. Remember me to all at Show time. Yours 'THE BREAKER'

The Boer War Monument in Windsor records the names of the three men who were killed in South Africa, George Jennings Dickson, Charles John Gosper and George Archie Montgomery. This area of the park was later renamed Memorial Park and a large monument honours those that participated in all wars.

Sport has always played a special part in the lives of the Windsor community. A cricket match between the visiting All England Eleven in 1882 was played against a team selected from players from the Hawkesbury and Nepean at Windsor. A special train conveyed about 1000 additional spectators to Windsor. The home team scored 61 with All England replying with 5 for 135.

Rugby Union, which had been introduced from England in the 1860s, was the first type of football played in the Hawkesbury. Rugby Union games were played in McQuade Park from at least 1896. Another code of football was introduced in NSW in 1907 and the first League team in Windsor was established by 1910. This became a popular sport, and the district won many premierships and produced many fine players.

Wisemans Ferry

Wisemans Ferry is opposite the Macdonald River, between the Bathurst and Trollope Reaches. This area was originally known as Lower Hawkesbury or Lower Portland Head. By the 1830s it was known as Wiseman's, as a tribute to Solomon Wiseman the emancipated convict who operated the ferry service across the Hawkesbury River. The locality eventually became Wisemans Ferry. Wisemans Ferry is adjacent to the Yengo National Park which covers an area of 153 254 hectares. Dharug National Park is 14 850 hectares.

Solomon Wiseman was a convict who arrived in 1806. He was a landholder on the Hawkesbury River as well as a merchant and shipowner. Wiseman also owned Cobham Hall which now forms part of the present day hotel. The ferry

Wisemans Ferry on the Hawkesbury River 1911 by John Henry Harvey 1855-1938. (State Library of Victoria)

service enabled Wiseman to supply provisions to the convicts and supervisors constructing the Great North Road. This area was a popular stopping off point for travellers as well as drovers with their stock coming and going from the north. When other access roads opened, the population diminished and the township almost faded away.

During the 1820s movement north to the Hunter Valley and Newcastle necessitated a road to be built. The Great North Road was surveyed in 1825 and completed in 1836. It was about 240 kilometres. It was a remarkable accomplishment on the part of the engineers, surveyors, overseers and the convict road gangs. Within the Dharug and Yengo National Parks about 40 kilometres of the original stonework, such as buttresses, culverts and bridges and road survives. It is one of Australia's heritage treasures and the Convict Trail Project is a group that co-ordinates all who have an interest in the road.

In 1927 Mr H. A. Rose of Coopernook was the first motorist to cross the Hawkesbury River on the new power driven punt at Wisemans Ferry. The crossing took 2 minutes as against 20 minutes on the old punt.

There were a number of citrus orchards at Yarramundi from the 1800s. Four generations of the Clemson's lived in the district. This label is from R. J. Clemson's Orchard. (June and Judy Clemson)

Yarramundi

Yarramundi is a scattered settlement located about four kilometres west of Richmond, on the way to Penrith. The first Europeans to reach the Hawkesbury in 1789 camped in the vicinity of the Yarramundi Lagoon and heard the nearby waterfall. The area is named after the Aborigine Yarramundi (also recorded as Yal-lah-mien-di and Yellomundee) who met the party led by Governor Phillip. A small group of the Boorooberongal clan met up with the group and three of them joined the party. They were recorded as Gombeeree, his son Yellomundee who had healing powers and grandson Djimba.

Charles Palmer and his family arrived in 1802 and were amongst the few free settlers in the colony at the time. They settled on a 100 acre grant near the lagoon. Other early settlers in this district were convicts Charles and Eliza Davis. Their son Joseph was a fencer from Yarramundi. He purchased most of his timber from the Kurrajong district and was responsible for many kilometres of slip-railing fences around the Richmond district. Rudolph Kroehnert, a migrant from East Prussia, arrived in 1854 and married Joseph's sister, Matilda Davis. Kroehnert had a shop here with Joseph Lowe in the 1850s.

Other pioneering families were the Timmins, Stinsons and Crowleys. The Howell family ran a flour mill at Yarramundi near the falls. Three blacksmith shops were recorded at Yarramundi in the early part of the 19th century. They were conducted by William Pearce, Edwin Harper and James Rider. In 1929 two local men Norman Farlow and Phillip Timmins were charged with using dynamite explosives to catch fish. They netted seven fish before being nabbed by the local police and were later fined £10 each.

Wisemans Ferry Hotel in the late 19th century.
(HCCLS)

A sylvan Hawkesbury scene photographed by Woodhill circa 1890. (HCCLS)

SELECTED

Back from the Brink: Blue Gum Forest and the Grose Wilderness / MACQUEEN (1997)

Bilpin: the apple country / HUNGERFORD (1995)

Bit of River History / CHRIS (1905)

Colo Wilderness / PRINEAS and GOLD (1978)

Cross Currents : historical studies of the Hawkesbury / POWELL (1997)

Darug and their neighbours : the traditional Aboriginal owners of the Sydney region / KOHEN (1993)

Disastrous Decade : Flood and Fire in Windsor 1864–1874 NICHOLS / (2001)

Early Days of Windsor / STEELE (1977, 1916)

Early Hawkesbury Settlers / HARDY (1985)

Ebenezer Schools 1810-1988 / BRILL (1988)

Exploring the Hawkesbury / JACK (1986)

Footsteps along the Ridge : the first 125 years of Kurrajong East Public School 1878-2003 (2003)

Forgotten Valley / NEVE (1982)

Good Old Days...reminiscences concerning the Hawkesbury district / FITZPATRICK (1900)

Government Schools of NSW 1848-1998 : 150 years / DEPT OF EDUCATION (1998)

Hawkesbury 1794-1994 (NICHOLS and BARKLEY (1994)

Hawkesbury Journey / BOWD (1986)

Hawkesbury Pioneer Register / HAWKESBURY FHG Vol. 1 (1994) and Vol. 2 (2001)

HRA and HRNSW

History of Lower Portland Public School 1867 – 1967

History of Pitt Town Vol. I and II / STUBBS (1983)

Home was here / LANG (1987)

BIBLIOGRAPHY

Kurrajong / WEBB (1980)

Lachlan Macquarie, Journals of His Tours in NSW and VDL (1979)

Last of the Logan: true adventures of Robert Coffin Mariner in the years 1854 to 1859…/ COFFIN (1941)

Macquarie Country / BOWD (1982)

Mosquito Fleet, Hawkesbury River Trade and Traders 1794-1994 / PURTELL (1995)

Mount Tomah Book / MT TOMAH SOCIETY (1987)

Newtown Streetscape study, 456-466 George Street, Windsor South / BARKLEY JACK (1998)

Oakville Public School Centenary 2000

Origins of names of streets, parks and features, Windsor / BOWD (1973)

Shut out of the world : the Hawkesbury Aborigines Reserve and Mission 1889-1946 / BROOK (1994)

The Ferry The Branch The Creek / DHARUG and LWR HAWKESBURY HS (2002, 1987)

Ups and Downs of an Old Richmondite / SMITH (1991)

Wilberforce Cemetery / McHARDY (2003)

Newspapers
Australian
Hawkesbury Herald
Sydney Gazette
Sydney Morning Herald
Windsor and Richmond Gazette
now *Hawkesbury Gazette*

Unloading hay at the railway station. (HCCLS)

INDEX OF PEOPLE

Pictorial History books are available in newsagencies and local bookshops or contact us at 02 9557 4367 or our website www.kingsclearbooks.com.au Email: kingsclearbooks@gmail.com Postal address PO Box 335, Alexandria NSW 1435

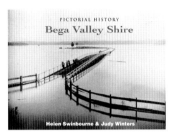

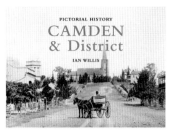
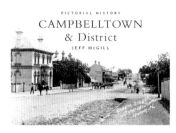

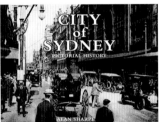
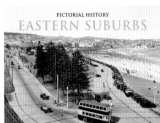

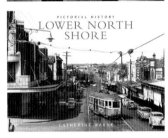

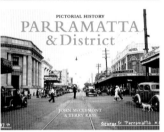

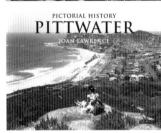

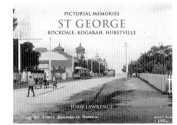
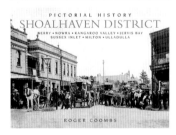

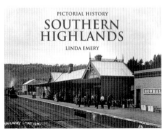
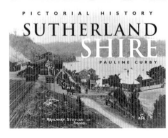
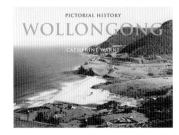